TRUTHVILLE TESTING

WALT MES

StayUp B Immortal Series

BALBOA.PRESS
A DIVISION OF HAY HOUSE

Balboa Press books may be ordered through booksellers or by contacting:

Balboa Press
A Division of Hay House
1663 Liberty Drive
Bloomington, IN 47403
www.balboapress.com
844-682-1282

ISBN: 979-8-7652-3892-9 (sc)

Print information available on the last page.

Balboa Press rev. date: 03/09/2023

Doctor Acknowledgement

I have been a Natural Doctor all my Life. Much experience. I had to learn. Was forced to learn. The reason I can Dr myself is cause I have info that is also backed by the Saints & Gods. Treatment that works the very 1ˢᵗ time cause it is potent, filled with Saint wisdom. God wisdom. I have dabbled with crystals, brass, marble, granite & jewels to name a few. But food grade H2O2 & Frankencense cause of 2012 end time energy shift (big changes even in the Schumann resonance) r the way now 2 go. Am well versed in natural healing. People do not evaluate for Purity. Good herbs poisoned with bad sky metals + fuel, etc & icides cannot heal. Nutrition is not there. Nutrition cant b utilized. Rather a poisoning occurs which u r not allowed. Purity is wat brings safety & Immortality energy. Healing is only possible with God positive energy. Ie: Purity.

In Atlantis crystals were heavily used but the 2012 energy shift has caused them mostly to weaken instead of helping. Even magnetic bracelets & many other things deter Holy Health now. Yes, Health is a Bible requirement. & 2012 is a new requirement for Living. We have 2 correct improper destructive energy so prevalent in society today & even in the Air. Cant even utilize Holy Air now without Dr Ox or H2O2 de poisoned. Food grade hydrogen peroxide. Is not ok 2 b exposed to these harmful energies.

Biofeedback & Touch For Health meridians document Truths about the body & negative emotions. Testing adds the finger & toe prints. & Spinal magnet. Emotions r shown in the arches & palms. Wen we put Self control or Soul above mind we see how to document these principles we kno. We learn 2 avoid food that does not Love us back.

With Truthville Testing we can see clearly how important electrolyte balancing is. & how important nonfat milk & a yolk is. Yolk is the food for the growing chick. Creates

Life itself. Is for Heart & Spine. Therefore brain. & we see how bad meat is. An egg white is meat. These r no theories but scientific fact wen we put Soul b4 mind. Is evidence that we find that saves Soul from separation & destruction. Saves nerves, Spine & brain for a Healthy & Holy Soul connection. Posture is an approximation of Soul connection. Of Soul safety.

Wat we build in Life governs also our afterLife. God demands we be strong. Is unfortunate demand of the Universe. U cant continue to grow organs & b human with weakness. Nor animal. Only the strong survive. Wat happens to the dogmatic Christian who believes in weak? B ye not Perfect. Follo the money. Who stands to gain? Christ said to b Perfect. Perfect energy so u dont bow down to sickness or BAD POSTURE. Law dictates u must b strong. 2 b or not 2 b. Wat did u reply 2 Mark Anthony? How many want the human vehicle? A human version with a Spine? I do & I hope u realize too & conquer weakness. Bcome Immortal by always doing good & right. Moral. Pure to the max. By staying Up in the human centers U CREATE A EUPHORIA THAT WILL TAKE U HIGHER & HIGHER TOWARD IMMORTALITY. Purity is necessary for that. Stay up B Immortal is not as hard as the dark want u to think.

Some learn 2 test right away. Others take a while but wat is important is u test everything. TAKE THE TIME. Save time out of error learning by doing. Incorporate Truthville Testing in ur Life. Save/rid months of destructive satanic energy taking u down. Paramahansa Yogananda guided me in this writing. Is from Paramahansa Yogananda or Saint John, the 1st of the 12. Is no option. Purity is a requirement to stay human. Do u see how far the world is off? Organs can only exist with a human Spinal Heart to nourish them. IS SCIENCE more important than dogma. No vice drama. Is unsustainable. Just the religion of good. I show the way that is necessary at this time. I have the blessing of access to the Father.

'Findin Joy pay 56. That is all life is. Tests.' (tests to b 5 fing(er) human. 6 is num for human. like Walmart logo.)

'We cannot control our thots but we can control our emotions if we chose to.'

'Others have thots but I think of God. God is the liberating force.'

'Just don't go into thots & have only pos(itive) emotions.'

Introduction-Testing is the way to Youth, to Truthsville

Want to learn to test food, sky, anything for corrupt toxicity that harms the Soul connection? Truthville is science, not religion. Science of ener(gy) These r the laws of creation that govern our Soul via the Spinal blueprint that we build. Walt is the most magnetic, beautiful & Pure person I have ever met. Wen u meet a Saint, u r changed forever. Such Charisma. Such Purity & Power. Learn to test & Dr urself by monitoring the Lifeforces. Then u can advance.

Reincarnation was taken out of the Bible at the 2nd council of Constantinople, Turkey centuries after Christ. The powerful do change Scripture for control of the people: 'There will only b 1 life cause we will send them to hell.''If there is only 1 life, theyll try harder' or 'We can con them better'. Is why it is better to get Truth of Scripture from the Saints. But they forgot to take out about Elija & Elias. In a former life He was a great Saint. But in the new life 'He came back but they knew Him not.' John the Bapitst Christ said was Elija therefore also Elias. 2 references of truth right in the present day Bible. Also, Mary Magdeline was no prostitute ever. Prostitutes do not have the ability to see a Resurrection. She was a Saint w ener above head. Was 1st to see the Resurrection. Prostitutes have Spinal ener in hell center at the base of Spine. There is evidence that She played a very signeficant role. But where r Her Books? Who suppressed them? The powerful write history. The books can now b found.

Walt was John Dee (13 July 1527–1608), the Original 007. There is a John Dee Society even now putting together His library. He spied for Queen Elizabeth who ruled unmarried. He would sign His name on notes to her as the hidden eyes for the Queen. OO for eyes & the cover over the eyes & down. A long top on the 7. Totally hidden eyes, the 7 was for hidden. 007. He had the greatest library in England of over

4,000 books. The next biggest, the University of Cambridge had 451. He continues that trend this life.. has every worthy metaphysical, health, Dr, money book.. any that is needed to live life. & most were written by Saints. Dee was navigator, alchemist, hermeticist, many many things. Changed nav by applying Euclidean geometry. Built the instruments to apply Euclid. Trained the 1st great navigators. Developed the maps. Charted new passasages. Translated Euclid & wrote the famous Mathematical Preface. Was Philosopher to Queen Elizabeth. Did her horoscope. Set her coronation date astrologically. She came to visit Him on her horse w her court to see His library. Dee coined the term British Empire. God wanted 1 language to unite the world. Dee was commissioned by Elizabeth to establish the legal foundation for North America. He developed a plan for the British Navy. In the British Museum r several items including a Seal, orb, & His conjuring table which contains the Enochian Alphabet He used as Angel language. Dee founded the Rosicrucians. Shakespeare depicted Dee as Prospero(to hope for the future) from The Tempest & also as King Lear. The 007 was the insignia Elizabeth also used for private messages betw(between) her Court & Dee. Wen the Spanish Armada loomed over the English Channel Dee said to just b still. Devastating storms destroyed the Spanish Fleet while the English waited. Dee lived God truth/harmony, not evil. Walt looks & acts like Dee, can control the weather many, many times at WILL for any need(even a breeze to cool), put bubbles over the house to keep neg(ative) ener out from s(tone) coxxyx people & add Ox(ygen) to a room. S refers to the stone/enemy magnet of the hate, fear lowest Spinal center, the coxxyx magnet at base of Spine that is so toxic/mark of the beast. Fear is not to b felt. Is a neg(ative) evil emotion. S can burst pipes/pipelines, break or damage a car or computer, burn/melt a human. They catch on fire. Walt lives w a silver spoon in His mouth that He deserves. Lives in the luxurious God vibration. Is loved by all, even animals who come 2 Him for His pos ener. Is savy, clever, rich acting, but moral, insightful, Powerful, pos, Blissful..., all good qualities. Has developed feeling far surpassing any woman where feeling is predominant.

Saint Walt, a Sita like Rajarsi Janakananda was the oldest of the 5 good Pandava Brothers in the Gita wen Paramahansa was Arjuna & Babaji was Krishna. They had much higher & more advanced atomic & other weapons in that higher descending age. & yes, civilation began in the west. Sitas r very great beings & help millions, even Heavenly bodies to stay Up. These r pearls, precious pearls of Wisdom that the greedy cant understand. Cant cast pearls b4 swine. They march to vice. It is not suggested to concentrate on Powers or who we were but it can b helpful to know who can help us advance. & we gain inspiration to advance. Rajarsi was the youngest Pandeva. The middle Pandavas had Final liberation who came back at this time to help us again. A crew coming again & again thru different religions to bring Truth & cast out dogma. Walt met 2 of Them in Their present body thru Intuition on the internet/realized Their significance. Has perfect intuition. The Gita is about the battle of good vs bad & the actual battles also happened.

We have 100% control of our emotions. We must use unpresidented effort to show this. Fly in only the pos emotions. React to ALL situations w pos emotions as Walt teaches. Regulate food intake avoiding ALL poi(son) & any vice cause of the sickness producing hell vibration it creates. We have the testing but need to use it in our life. Can w(with) testing rule out the heavy vice & vice equated ener. Will help us do everything in the God vibration which advances us to safety. This book needs to b studied until all is applied. Is filled w common sense from a Sita, liberated for millions of years & has disciples all over the place. Is the way to safety. This will give us freedom so that we dont lose our Soul. Purity & Virtue r a high frequency which lifts us in Spine. Will Levitate us so we can walk on water. Lifts our Spinal karma/ener. The Spine shows the measure of karma we have. How much pos ener. Testing is the only way for scientific success no matter wat religion. Cause all religions tell us we must fly in the pos emotions of the upper Spine. Testing will show us proper nutrition. No guess work. Is the way to pos ener.

Dr Ox(explained later) & Franken can immensely help us counter the poi & pain in life. A shotgun to kill the enemy vibration. It raises Spinal ener. Air is missing in our diet & is much more imp(ortant) than food which is 99% poi anyway. & metal/water conduct. Let us not conduct a bad frequency. Everything has ener. Wifi, fone, 5g, internet, all emf, poisons, metal/liquid conducting these, the spraying of the sky. All have a very neg evil ener. We can build Purity by using God common cents raising ener earning good Spinal karma. God money. We take the Spinal ener to the hereafter. Fasting is necessary to limit the poi intake. Wen fasting, our old Soul has to make child tendancies wash dishes(clean up ignoring hunger) after movie distraction.. food. They have 2 learn to work. Learn to fast washing the dishes we eat w to start clean for next meal. Improve our ability to test. Testing is necessary to get all our body & Soul needs. Soul has to have pos ener. There r pos vibrations like the Galactic Ellegion cd that heals; the dvd vibration(does not heal but does not hurt) but not the metal player usually/metal will conduct the evil in the air; very many Up Saints can also help &

heal us; & Up Spir(itual) brass like in Atlantis can help fix weakenings(not crystals) if we dont have neg Spinal ener. It is really up to us if we r Up or down. Some may have to give the greatest of commitment to change the downward repulsive flow. But then u r Free. Bound by Up.

It is hoped that we each save ourselves from destruction so that each can afford the same level of wonderment in the herafter as we do now. Healing can b had just by being Up. Healing from anything. The Saints r more eager to give it than we r to ask. But God's law has to b honored, Truthville lived.

Walt's mission in life is to show people how to stay Up. Of all the 7th people He introduced me to & all others that I know(100s), He is the only one in the world that I know that knows this art completely. Others go Up & down s(stone/enemy red magnet). Saints have a very hard life to set an example for others to follow. The thots r there just like radio waves. We tune in to learn how to do it.. how to escape from a seemingly impossible problem making it into an easy to do task.

One can misinterpret His intention but Walt is locked in the Bliss of God. But to b in the Bliss of God, one has to have 100% Wisdom & no ego. It is not easy to b all in the 7th above the head(halo). Many times He would tell us that to stay Up at times it took the greatest effort. That it would have been much easier & much less painful to just go down. But Walt stayed Up never taking the easy way out. Cause no shortcuts exist. Walt is a stickler for detail. Hundreds of 7th people I know & They do not have all Their ener in the 7th. Truthsville is Wisdom of how to succeed to raise our vibration. It is Bliss, Love, Joy, Peace, Happiness, Cheerfulness. Walt is 100% in that Bliss & it enabled Him to expand into infinity/God the Father. All the ener was above His head very quickly once he developed HOW to STAY UP in the 1980s. There r many Saints Up but They dont have the concept of wat it means. Even in the Angelic Heavens. So They like us go down at times confronted by problems. But Walt even in action is UP. He reacts w Bliss to the problem. Can go into Nirbikalpa Samadhi/Christ's state at will. His breath stopped but yet He can walk up & down stairs. Highest Samadhi in activity. 'These that I do, u can do & greater' Christ did not reveal all His powers. He also said that He died daily. Stopping the Heart in breathlessmess is that death. Saints can even walk on water. Walt came to help Paramahansa Yogananda who is called one of the most influential people of the 20th century & Walt is.

All Saints in Heaven no matter the religion understand & work together headed by Sananda who is Christ whom we know. Walt helped Paramahansa as John Dee(Original 007) wen Guru(Master/enlightened teacher) was Shakespeare. Shakespeare got away from His work to spend time w God in Dee's home. But this is the beauty of fully Up Saints. They come again & again as a crew in each new mission to bring Truth cause man usually turns it into dogma & judges others. Walt makes Truth, makes Paramahansaji's life & teachings real.

Walt has been a Saint for millions of years. Lives in tune w the Gurus. W the liberated Beings. Walt goes out only once a week yet there is always plenty Oxygen at all times never opening to a closed garage. Is tested but never low. He adds it in med(itation). Walt controls the weather.. every Dr or Dentist made weeks b4 or a friend's need, the Air gets good. He silently prays to God in activity(noone ever knows) & Air gets good. & wen the need is over, it immediately gets bad. I witnessed this many times.

Walt is a very famous person in the Bible. One that they forgot 2 take out about reincarnation. Not Saint John, the chief disciple, a very great Soul. Walt throughly loved in that life too. He gives to the world in this life the key. Exactly wat advances & wat sends one to hell. By scientific means one can become Immortal & also Dr oneself. Walt helps many people who want to live by His example. Pick up His thot waves by always doing right asking God to show the way to complete Purity.

Walt is eager to help & heal all, always full of ener giving Love. One does not need to belong to a particular religion to receive. After all these high Saints come thru all the religions. A crew to guide. God does not create religions. There is only one God & we can get access to healing from Anyone w abilities in the Company of God, any UP Healer in the Co of Good. They r all together in the Heavenly realms & 1 in principle as boots on the ground. Can ask any UP Santa(originally Saint Nick)/Saint at the north pole of the Spine Dressed in purpl courage. Never a red suit. Is a commercial creation to further bad. Walt showed me how to Love. He always puts Staying Up & giving Love 1st no matter wat.

This is the most imp book Walt wrote. Had to make sure every sentence, every paragraph was Walt's not rewording wat He wrote, a huge task necessary to do for His mission/why He came. He helps millions. He can help all of us & liberate us too, a foreman or supervisor in the Co of God. Of good. He reports to the manager or CEO. Is a hierachy. To get Final liberation one has to liberate 6 people. It is hard to find someone who can help us cause we dont have the ability to see who is perfect. Many chose a religion thinking someone in that religion has to help them but many times, most times they dont find access to wat they need. Their high God being tho perfect does not talk back to them. But wen we have perfection b4 us in our life, that is a rare opportunity that needs to b taken advantage of so we dont fall 2 hell. A Hindu may think well, go thru Krishna yet they cant make contact. After all that is a long time ago & u have to have powerful will to access, to get them to talk back. why not utilize the perfect ones who arent anymore Chritian or Hindu but r in this present world where They r helping again? After all it is CEO Christ who sent Them. The Saints, like us go thru many different bodies in many different countries. Most find it impossible 2 believe yet it is true. Reincarnation was in Bible early on. So will it b us who get liberated? Who put in effort to create good tendancies? Or will we become a fallen used unhappy ghost cause we did not apply ourselves? Did not steer. One life lived then misery. Finally knowing the terrible Truth. But this Supervisor developed the method to Stay Up in the Spine, then lived in the Final Liberation state. So it is imp to know who can help cause many r down & cannot but in Walt we have full knowledge that He can help. Walt can talk us if we r receptive/talk thru us. We think it is us thinking but we r puppets. Saints can have multiple bodies & do. They can b formless too. R in every speck of creation. So they can help us if we try to do right.

We can argue & have our own thots but that wont get us where we want to b. Many go to hell being their own person. So it easily could b a dark overlay.. neg Spinal magnets. Wen we reject God's pos ener, we will not find God or Happiness that way. No matter wat we call God but the pos ener in head is the goal of all. Pos emotions so to b Cheerful & Blissful, etc. We have to follow those that r Up to get a winning play. Become the pos ener. Walt is a great aid cause He is Up. He healed Mom & others of cancer, strokes, blood poi & many other things. Walt mirrors the person He is interacting w just like Parmahansa Yogananda did. Totally w the other person. A best friend. Noone realizes He has been liberated for millions of yrs. Walt just acts like a friend, always hiding His greatness. He takes me on again & again & destroys wat He can of my bad actions/karma changing me forever. Does not heal Himself. That is wat They do. Heal others.

- the Editor

Truthsville Testing by Walt Mes

Written in plain English, a much needed shorthand to update the outdated, saving time & paper, more valuable than anything. Tho not perfect; it is a rough draft, a trend to develop.

'The one who sizes up all deterrances thru testing will b rich & safe in God Luxury. In Bliss Cheerful beyond measure.'

This is not a religion but facts to help ANYONE who wants help or Truth. I mention certain Saints cause I write from my experience. There is only one religion of right or Truth. These r the laws that will help anyone b in their top Spinal center. One above where they have stabalized on so they can advance to the next center. It is the way to health destroying all disease. To keep the Soul & body in a perfect state of Joy, Bliss, Peace which r a part of God. It is a wonderful feeling to have strong fings(fingers)/lifeforces. W strong lifeforces, we get Up better which helps the fings even more. No disease can touch us if our fings r strong cause our elimination & every system is working optimally. Our Heart & brain then get the ener they need. The eyes then look alive.

If we get Up in the higher centers destroying all lower magnets we can much quicker evolve. Takes Dropping the ego all at once. Usually 8(b4 2012), it now is 3 yrs. If we r 4th, we can attain the 5th w some neg magnets. But to get from 5th to the 6th or from 6th to 7th, we need to abolish the neg magnets for a safe trip up to God. All power is up in the 7th above the head. The ener is finer & so more imp to abolish all neg ener/habits. Have a good base. There r many stories of very high people falling & burning their nerves. Some r reborn w autism or major Spinal problems. But now fallen ones will fall all the way to hell cause of 2012. God's cleaning house. We need a good base so we dont fall to oblivion. In Angelic realm or the Heavens all r skinny cause that is necessary for totally UP. Virtue & morals r necessary even more. These r wat we should do. Many were born

6th in this life, had experiences of God in the 7th but lost their pension burning out the 6th fine ener. Now they cant relate to that pos experience being stuck in food or vice. Wen 1 burns out a center, there is a vacancy there. They keep their Spir experiences but they cant feel the Bliss anymore or the higher pos emotions.

W 2012 & the change in frequency, we could make it to safety in 12 yrs(was 32 b4 2012) if we worked extremely hard against the flow. Raise neg ener to Heart(Spinal Heart betw shoulderblades) w throat open in the 1st 3(We can b in the center we developed & stabalized in plus 1(Heart to Throat for instance). Then stabalizing in Spinal throat the 2nd 3. 6th is open then, the Spir Eye(medulla(neg)/betw eyebrows(pos)) which we can capture, can stabalize in Spir Eye & open the 7th in 3 more. Then we progress in the 7th & stabalize(3 yrs Up 2 stabalize) in the 7th. The 7th will 1st be neg flat on head, then pos flat on head, later pos above head as we expand out into infinity. Once stabalized there in the 7th, most karma is gone & our 3 lower centers radiate pos. Those will never fall to hell again ever. While many r going extinct, let us march forward to success, to freedom from the dark rule who fills us w poison to take away our Soul. We have to have the Heart center strong to keep our Soul, ie. no lower ener. A Saint in the 7th can forget the rules & burn out the nerves but They will never lose the 7th or have any neg centers below the Heart. Having worked out most of their bad actions/karma, They stay in God's main Grace. Their neg centers r the Heart, Throat & Spir Eye cause they should b above the head only. These facts can b seen in pics of the Spine. Saints, Healers, Prophets? Is all the same. The variance or advancement is shown in the Spine. Their attainment. There r Saints w Final liberation that r locked in the head or above. Others can go down to Heart chakra but not lower. The human body is a very desired vehicle but who takes care to keep it? Who puts staying Up 1st? Who knows wat it means?

6th w 7th open is a very critical time to b right in all we do. It is a very magnetic refined ener if we dont have magnets in the lower centers that brake us. Hands collapsed w a left-right lifeline in palm is a sign of neg ener. Ener should flow thru & out the tips like Healers where a long life lifeline goes toward the fingers. Ener is not blocked. We establish the oppo habit to change. Is not a matter of overcoming but of doing right activities till it holds. B an observer of wat u go thru.

The 4th needs to concentrate on Happiness & Cheerfulness in the Spinal Heart betw the shoulderblades. Love will b too close to sex usually to b successful. 7th should concentrate on feeling Bliss later expanding out in Bliss. The 5th & 6th should Love the Joy in Spir Eye a bit lower than betw eyebrows keeping the attention there 24/7. Love is powerful. If we concentrate on Pure Love long enuf we can even materilize the Saints & Gurus(Indian for Master/better vibration). Same w Bliss & Cheerfulness. Especially cause of 2012 ener beamed Happy, Joy, Bliss, etc will bring more success than Love. Is cause of all the poison, all the vice equated things like bad frequencies, poi air, etc. The pos emotions r the key 2 access God. Why not then just b pos & help? Help the body by testing wat u give it. Not abusing but being a kind king ego. Have Up tendancies. A Mr Wisdom & a Joyful Loving Ma. We have to b kind & loving to others to b Up: Please forgive me if I offended u. Did not intend to. Just want u to know my Love is there no matter wat u do. Have to understand & b giving or it will come back on us just like a boomerang as a bad magnet. The neg emotions & even the slight neg emotions can only exist in the lower centers. Being heavier they exist in navel or belo hense all the rules. Takes ener down in avoid zone as if we were practicing vice. The rules r just to protect us from losing our Heavenly Father, pos emotions & health. To have a good base for our bodily house.

Scoliosis & other Spinal problems, ms, alz is a sign of neg ener which causes Oxygen starvation. If no ener in upper Spine, body is not getting Ox. It is surprising how many people think they can live wo Air. But Ox, Hydro & Nitrogen r really Holy bringing Life. Not only do They k ill cancer, They will reverse ANY disease. Now w aluminum, raw face(from a corrupt ener) fuel & rat poi in the air, the Air is corrupt, changed forever. No more Pristine, even in the mountains. People must stand up & demand Purity from the 1%. Big business should protect us, not eat us. If we have inflammed areas or Free radicals which we do, we need also Frankencense that kil ls inflammation. After Franken on Spine & brain, vertebrea will crack easier. That is how powerful this inflammation fighter is. Also pain.. instantly better. & healing is speeded up tremendously. Hydrogen k ills Free radicals even in brain. This is vital: to fight poi & nerve toxins that will hurt our access to our Soul. Poi cannot bring health & Life but only sickness & death. Soul separation if it continues too long. Even if u get into a closed car w heater closed off takes 20 min(utes) for the spraying of the sky to fall belo nose so u can take off ur mask. Italy made a film on the spraying of the sky being w a r on humanity. The internet calls it gen ocide of the people. Aluminum, rat poi, raw jet fuel... It is not possible for us to Love if we hurt ourselves & others w our down magnet wen we have the means to b Up. Cannot breathe the enemy air 2nd hand smoke & mirrors but God Pristine Air. We can help all kinds of people, make big money doing it but it wont keep us out of trouble w God, our Soul & our health later in life & after death. A mask is necessary to not become extinct. Mortals cannot inhale or take in poi & expect to conquer. A sick body or Spine is the temple of the enemy to wreak havoc in. Many looked back to vice or were oblivious to vice equated poi & lost the opportunity to continue on. Wat keeps us out of trouble is being up in our center we stabalized in(Spinal Heart betw shoulderblades or above for humans/7th for Immortal Saints). We dont give Love wen we r down but r more concerned w the world. Down ener destroys the connection to the Soul eventually being accused of Soul suicide for a hell sentence. We r more concerned w our likes & dislikes or our false beliefs. 'I dont need help. Im good.' All while inhaling rat poi & the like. So testing is 100% Wisdom & brings the 7th magnet for us all in this life if we follow God's pos ener. We cut out the neg crippling ener. The biggest source is the spraying of the sky. Even a 4th centered person can stabalize in the 7th moving up one chakra every 3 years if they follow these rules: TEST EVERY BITE. FIX EVERY WEAKENING. Right action is necessary to spiral up.

Routers should not b used in the home. Landline phone is safer than cell. No fone is ideal. Then u can have a line to God. Can communicate via email at library or borrow someone's phone for absolutely necessary things. Use library wifi, etc as little as possible. Dont b addicted to the internet. Is vice equated. Get absolutely necessary communication & leave. Weigh if it is really necessary to have internet in home w weakening of the wired connection. At any moment metal can go to s wrecking ur magnet. So many bad frequencies. Haarp in Alaska controls weather world wide. Pulses emf that hurt Heart. Used to more than now. People probably complained. On their website they say they will control the weather by 2025. They already do.

Metal tools & other metal can go to s easily. best to keep oside(outside) lower than urself. No metal is allowed in the home. Nails r calked/siliconed. Keep metal out of the house maybe 25 ft away on a board lower than ur house half ft above the Earth. On the board u may find a lil(little) stainless steel egg yolk cooking cup wrapped in something face free so bugs stay away, ur keys hidden, hammer, pruning shears, nails or watever few metal tools u need (as in building) & can get by w. Have metal tools that have 3 uses(saw for cutting wood or sickle weeds for path or 2 cut calk tube in half to apply w wooden stick). Paint & pliers that u arent using usually maybe even further down hill. Have as lil as possible even of necessary things. U can hose off tools(rain will do) & other things on the board so they wont b so faced & go down as easily. Sometimes u will find they r s & u will have to toss them. So buy them wen u need them. But washing them will save u from major face getting on u. Will help u to stay Up. Chemicals r s & affect things they r on, even u. Is why one should wear gloves to touch things. Chemicals & poi r everywhere. Will also find on the board at times candles that have metal to hold the wick. But tape measure can b replaced w rope. Cordless drill would need 2 b much further away. U want to avoid potential weakenings cause at any time metal can go 2 s cause of the destructive freqs in the air.

Better to bury ur spare keys in a jar, hide ur camera oside in a plastic box w lid. In car if u absolutely have 2 have it, better to keep metal in trunk.

We r not allowed to hurt others by being weak ourselves, being in the s. Is cruelty valuing objects over people. It is our duty to raise our Spinal ener for others & ourselves. Help others & our own tendancies bringing them to full grown adults. Adult habits. 'I write w a purpl pen. Each tendancy has that ener, then I advance. Am one past my stabalized chakra.' We can Dr ourselves. It is really very simple. Is doing everything the right way. Proper xrcise as in my stories book(Dr Ropes story), a straight Spine always, bending back raising the ener & keeping Spine healthy is the way to safety. Sleeping on back will not block ener from going up/advancing. This is wat karma is. & it can change fast if one is not vigilent. Have to brace ur back/sleep on back & always even while dancing have a straight Spine. Proper dancing as in the Heavens increases circulation. This is very much stressed in the East. Is like a wood stove. If pipe goes straight up, smoke can too. If there is a kink & it goes sideways as wen we sleep on side, smoke will not go up as much. Same principle. The 'smoke' has to go up completely to make it. 2 not devolve. W all the chemicals, we have mostly kinks. We will need all the help we can get. Many Drugs r in today's food & toxic environ. We cant b here & there & everywhere as on vacation. We must work very hard. Process every thot that comes 2 mind. Discern where it is coming from.

Throw out the s b4 it takes other things to s. If possible park a car far from house & others. Can go 2 s. S is trash for everyone. The science of ener has to b honored & lived. We dont overcome, we turn on the Light by Light & right actions that become habit. In here r the ways to b good to our body. Being a kind ruler of our bodily kingdom. Relaxation, moderation & keeping body Dry at night r extremely imp for success.

Purity is needed, the oppo(site) of poi. Block the impurities. The frequency of this 'Air', of Dr Ox(food grade H2O2) & also Franken is the way in this poi world to b

11

w God despite the impurities. Wen doing Dr Ox it is imp to lay awhile after u put ur ft up. That will give it time to soak in & do the work. Better take a bit less if cant hold. Feet up raises Spinal ener by draining blood out of legs. Is advancement of the Soul cause it raises Spinal ener. Cant force urself to overcome. That is the dark talking. The way is to turn on the Light in ur bodily home by utilizing/'eating' good frequencies like food grade Hydrogen Peroxide/Dr Ox & Franken, filtering the air w a mask that strains out the finest/most while also covering EVERY INCH, testing the food. Many masks r not tight enuf around the ears letting u breathe the trash. But we can bcome(become) great metal smiths straining metal out of our lungs, body & protecting our skin, throwing out metal in our home. It is trash. The Saints & Healers r God's helpers. R surcharged w this healing ener, w God's high vibration. This is a great aid to advancement. Is necessary to advance. Is wat God wants. To reach out for the good frequencies so u can Drop the bad. Then all is Happy, Delight & all the other pos good frequencies. Joy, Cheerful, Bliss... Wen we make an A in school on a test, we incorporate all knowledge for that A. Not just one philosophy. To pass the test of Life is same same. Use our brain 100% to take good from all we learn using common sense. Wen we want to do God's will, the bad will b overridden cause God's power is immense, can think thru us & take over so we r safe. We gave Him permission by choosing right.

I have a scale for testing of 0 to 21 where 21 is totally good. UU(oo oo) or trace 12 -20. Medium bad (uu shi)6-11. Shi or real bad if it is 2 - 5. Off the scale bad is 0-1.

I eat totally good(21). All I can find that tests totally good I get & only some of it I eat. I go to 3 or 4 grocery stores on shopping day while the Air is good & usually can find totally good milk & juice at one of them but many times it is trace or off the scale bad. My diet is limited but all encompassing. Batches vary. One batch could just b trace bad. This my family eats. Mine has to b totally good cause of the 24d poisoning. The next batch can b off the scale bad. Batches vary so one has to test buying some e(xtra) if it is good. Mom could have medium bad cause she grew up on a farm w no chemicals(1920s) but I got her trace or totally good. w slight exposure to chemicals as a child, one could handle trace. Testing lets us kno wat the body can handle.

Wen we r Up in the higher centers, God thru the Saints can heal us cause we used our freewill to hold on & b Up. If Spir healing ener is transmitted & we go down, it actually hurts us cause of the Spir ener being forced to vibrate negatively. If this happens there r ways to dissapate the xtra Spir ener: talking, keeping eyes open & xrcise. Gets ener out of Spine. This is most imp to keep moving so that the bad ener stays out of Spine & in muscles rather. Also the riddance of liquid helps to not transmit the bad magnet. Liquid & metal conduct. But thru all this b & act Happy, Love the Joy or feel Bliss. The pos healing ener was more pos than usual so is also magnified in the lower centers. We reduce the amount by these techniques. Pos ener touching neg centers shorts out like a car battery eventually. So is imp to stay Up. We must inspire ourselves. Surround ourselves w right activities. The brain's job is to police. Dr Ox can help w that cause ur concentration & memory r improved. The God tendancy needs to inject old man Wisdom/ignorance tendancy w i o dine (I oh Thine)! We will also get better testing results wen Up. These days since 2012 the Spir ener is unavoidable so we must tow the line now or lose everything. Dont humpty dumpty sitting on the fense. We must choose right. The Shumann Resonance of 1987 & now is totally different. Divine ener is beamed to Earth. Things that didnt matter, matter now. The Bible says let the dead bury the dead. Is cause of same principle. Those w neg vibrations in Spine are dead to God's world in the upper Spine. Dead to the pos emotions, Soul & healing ener. God's hands r tied if we are in the forbidden zone. They cant heal us cause we could not handle the pos ener. Would hurt us.

In the Etheric Heavens liberated Saints access many different dimensions. They know everything even tho u never told them. They live on the Sun in the 9th dimension. Sun is 9D. Lifts us. why we see Green, the color of the Heart where we should b at least if the enemy was not poisoning us/pulling us down. Or blue, indigo or purpl. Others live in other Etheric Realms like the Angelic Realms. Or the Pleiades Heavens. The Creator Gods who work for the 1 God have a 6th lil fing cooresponding to the Spiritual eye, The Single eye of intuition & Light cause of Their advancement. Is a mansion for only liberated Beings. Why would God allow negativity there? Would hurt the Gods. So u have to walk ur talk & get the Miracles 1st.

Wen we r fasting, Saints who r Up can dispel the fallen from our bodies. We all have them. Can tell by our not 100% right actions. The fallen 'amebas' get into our bodies thru ingesting poi. Dispelled, we r Up better. Fasting on liquids or water tho better than nothing could expose us to chemicals & we would not get nutrition. But if we test carefully, filter(keep stored where metal cant hurt u. grounded 1/2 ft above Earth far away oside where it cant transmit emf. wrap in sheet rubber? Test.) w accuracy, it can b a good time to rinse body w filtered distilled H2O2 since u may not b getting much liquid if the neg magnets allow it. Ie, if it tests. Most water in store is polluted making almond & similiar milks polluted. Vegans have a good goal. Is just the poi of our world & ourselves. We have to deal w the poisoning. Also Calcium from cow is the only option that the body can utilize. That fat can b skimmed from. Milkfat is not good.

20-30 min after Laminine can drink wat tests ok. 45 min or so after Laminine wen yolk tests, can test more filtered distilled since u r skipping juice for ketosis & milk cept maybe a swallow or 2 to balance pills if it tests. Fasting is a way to get rid of the poi metals that r piled up perhaps even showing gray on ur skin. All water needs to b filtered, even distilled from store for Drinking & Dr Ox. Containers wash out w very hot water 5-6 times & a soap maybe. Rinse the soap out very well w hot. Germs can exist in hot water heaters so finish w a cold rinse. Dry pores of skin will take longer to deface(from a corrupt ener/facecream chemicals & a conglomeration of all transient corrupt chemicals) & u cant use the hotest water. Face chemicals r very toxic, is in all food & anything ever touched & more. Soaks thru paper, cardboard & cotton but not plastic & synthetic fabrics. Makes u feel sluggish like u cant hardly move or do stuff. Cause u r poisoned. May have to finish w 1 or 2 soaps b4 it tests ok. Only way to get face out of ur mouth is swish a couple min w a bit of baby shampoo, etc that tests. Then spit. Repeat for trace face. Then once or twice more for totally good. We found also Polmolive & All detergent that tested good. Never Tide. Is as toxic as dole. If u get splashed or hit something accidently & cant use water, u can use a half of a small paper towel to dab up the face throwing it down immediately b4 it soaks thru to ur baggie. Take another, dabbing more. Use a lot. B sure to Drop towel fast cause towels soak face instantly so u dont get it on ur baggie. Depending on how much u got faced, keep this up till towel tests ok but dont hold it while testing. Set it down on a non faced bag. May even need more than 3 towels/quite many. Getting face off quickly will keep it from soaking into skin. This will help magnet so more will test good at mealtime. Hot water will work faster than towels. Wet hands that get faced r easier to deface than dry. The water keeps the face from soaking in quickly. Oily things will need soap. The face chemical from facecream, raw jet fuel(spraying of the sky), nana poison & etc is greasy.

Wen buying fold top sandwich bags to separate u from face in home, the boxes usually r very s. So if u buy the best u can find, carefully opening them putting them in a non faced bag, u can pick out the obvious s trashing them. Hopefully there r many that r ok to use, 10 or greater on the scale of 0 to 21. Wen buying food, touch fridge handles, etc where others usually dont touch. This is a good way to keep gloves trace face if u also touch real bad areas like the car steering wheel thru a baggie(gloved hand protected by baggie to keep glove trace face). Keeping gloves trace has the advantage that the face is not affecting ur fings/lifeforces like major face. Also keeping clothes good will help magnet. Faced clothes affect the centerline in front, Spine & head. Also palms, fing prints, arches & toe prints.

The face chemicals take ener to our lowest chakra. Face mixed in w food cannot burn off. Face on a hotplate burner usually does. Getting face on clothes makes the clothes more prone to go to s. I sit on clean plastic wen I sit down like at a bank. At the dentist I put plastic over the top of the dental chair to keep face off my neck. I wear a shirt that does not absorb face & wash the jeans & shirt wen I get home. Face does not go thru the jeans to face my skin for several hours. Would b very hard not to face the bottom half in a dentist chair.

But fasting on mostly nothing(some Dr Ox, a Yolk(or 2 if it tests), spoon flax oil, couple swallows milk for pills) can heal u much quicker of the stiffness from the poi. Test all. Knee, shoulder & other problems could b the stiffness of poi instead of lack of pulp/collagen. We have to b able to handle the Spir ener to make it. Fasting is key to get Purity. Dr Ox & Franken u cant do wo(without). Is not like nutrition. Cause they fix the Spinal ener. Get the purest 35% u can find & use it daily & interday(1/2-2 1/2%. Use it thruout the day or am & pm for success. Is vital medicine. The body cant do wo protection from coxxyx energy, toxins, wo Air. So test to see wat u can have.

The problem w fasting on liquids is u r exposing urself to poi. Wen Heart fing says I need liquid for low blood pressure(4th fing/respiratory) then take a bit. After the fast one is more capable of finding Pure enuf pulpy orange juice & organic nonfat milk cause one is Up better & also needs food(best time to shop). Unless u can test very well, avoid commercial food, 24d & hormones as much as possible by buying tested nonfat organic milk. Stay in balance w electrolytes for optimal Up & good lifeforces. Out of balance causes one to go down some & is enuf to make the nerves react/burn. Juice in a fast will take you out of ketosis fairly easily bringing hunger back but u can balance a couple swallows milk w pills that test. & some pills like NAC have sodium. Dont take inorganic calcium. Cannot b utilized. Body can do ok wo milk during the fast. The cow strains the milk for the calf but milkfat does not test good & clogs the arteries. It makes one gain weight which causes a down toxic magnet. Most bodies cant handle so much fat. Fat deadens the pan(creas) which raises blood sugar. Overdo fat & ull have also a galbladder indigestion problem later in life. So cow, not goat milk. Wen u get very much xrcise, ur fat intake ability goes way up. 1 yolk per day or meal w moderate xrcise but 6 yolks in 1st meal & only once a day wen hrs/all day of xrcise. Testing will show u wat u can have. Liquid conducts electricity which if one has down magnets, needs to b avoided. Dont conduct bad electricity if u want to live. But dry food adds poison. Wet washes out poi. Get rid of the xtra weight by limiting liquids & dry. Lanky the body & Spine need. The Angels r lanky for a reason.. to b UP.

The effect fat has on body has been revealed thru testing as has everything in this Book. Is not theory but Truth. Truthville.

On fat one can do largely wo omega 6 & olive oil even but these should b tested. Omega 3 is vital to b Up, for Heart & brain. The Heart needs us to eat omega 3 so Spine can get up best possible. Otherwise there is a tremendous strain on the Heart if we r down. Franken(allow some of ur fat for franken) also is needed for Up, inflammation, Oxygen, nerves, Spine, brain & pain. These taken care of take a burden off the Heart. Wen u get proficient at testing, u will see that the body knows wen it needs a certain oil including olive oil & omega 6. But we get some omega 6 in chia seeds. Too much fat or poi will crack feet w a high blood sugar problem. Anything that sets off diabetes fairly strongly. Test spices to lower if high. Many spices lower high blood sugar. Even aloa vera if u find non s. Tea tree oil or oregonol can heal the feet cracks, fungus or atheletes foot. Also parasites. They r good for teeth & gums too. Fat deadens the pancreas so unlimited or more than 4-5 bites or spoons a day is more than body needs or wants unless u get very much xrcise. Body cant handle more & can do fine on 2 fat per day. Fat on skin is largely unneeded & prevents us from getting our imp omega 3 & Lecithin to b Up. That should come 1st. Dr Ox will help keep the skin young not adding to fat intake keeping the magnet better by raising ener which naturally keeps us young. Tea tree oil & Franken can b used on face for healing the worst areas(but away from eyes) along w Dr Ox. Test Franken, tea tree, oregonol, all. But this fat accomplishes several goals like omega 3s.

Expulsion by Saints of the fallen amebas(a kinder word) wen one is fasting gives one their will back. But u have to xrcise it, a new concept. R not used to it. The fallen is a good reason not to breathe the spraying of the sky inside or oside. Some heaters pull in the oside Air like ac does. It takes 12 hrs for the fine pollution to fall to the floor.

The aluminum, barium rat poi, raw jet fuel, lead, radioactive strontium 90, etc. is dumped out of the wings. Industrial pollution falls in 12 hrs also. These fallen amebas inhaled or otherwise gotten into the body is why people have trouble controlling food. Amebas bully their desires onto people having nothing more to lose. They keep u from steering ur life properly & can hold a person's brain for ransom. Food(is drugged) is like sex these days. Same effect. Cant mess w appl in middle of bodily garden. Do we tune in God/Saint radio waves or the enemy & his amebas? Wen we dont do the will of God we r most likely doing the will of the fallen. In the beginning of breathing the oside Air or if we r young, we dont notice a bad effect not being able to feel the ener in the lowest Spine, at least not all the ener down there.. But as we inhale more & more, our metabolism will not function as properly. We can even turn grey in places as the skin tries to eliminate the aluminum, etc. & we will lose abilities, maybe even Spinal levels. But chemicals r piling up whether we see or dont see them. Wen our cell buckets get full of trash, then sickness will show itself. But will show up on the elimination current, the thumb right away. But people's will is being overridden by the neg amebas. people dont realize this & eat thinking it is them wanting the food even tho they want to b strong. But wen something is stolen like eating food that does not test good, how is it billed? We pay w the downward neg flow of ener creating health issues that we could have avoided & slows down the chance for advancement & Happiness to a crawl or slower or backward toward devolvement. The red end pops the rest.. destroys the upper human centers making them inoperable & vacant if ener is too long in the red coxxyx. If we harbor the enemy frequency b4 death, we most likely will join him in the afterlife. Ener doesnt dissappear or change just cause u die. It goes somewhere. This is basic science that the Saints also realize.

The Saints, the creator Gods in charge of us r more ready to help us than we r to ask(Let Us make man in Our image). U can accidently hit urself in head w a hammer & if u r doing right like fasting, They can heal u instantly b4 u can think to ask or experience any pain. Their job is to help us escape the injustice of the evil ones who abuse freewill. These good r the Eloheim of the Bible, the Himalayan Yogis of the East, the Creater Gods, the Galactics. They created us. They can do most anything. Can b as big or as small as They want. As heavy or as light as They want. They see into the future & know all. See beyond death. R in every speck of creation(Omnipresent & Omnipotent). Can reach Them anywhere. They can create Mountains & make them dissappear. Can turn paint scribbles into faces. They can interact in the formless state(God the Father state), can make us realize our errors & change our circumstances if we give them that power by behaving & asking. They can control thru others our circumstances if we misbehave. & complete power to alter if it is our will to have Them discipline us for misbehaving. & reward for behaving. They can discipline us even if we dont want Them to. They can pick out the exact amount of nails or shingles u need for the day giving them a good non s(stone or enemy) magnet. Can hold off the rain till u get in the car. Have people rush to help u wen u do right.. solve ur problem, give money, anything.

People dont realize all these things they do or foods/nutrition they eat to replace Oxygen wen they can go right to the source. Food grade Hydrogen Peroxide or H2O2 35%(Dr Ox) mix w distilled H2O that u filtered. We dont get Air! & coxxyx ener does not process Air or liquid properly. Lack of Air causes pain & disease. One should not need a Dr. For Dr Ox mix to 1/4 - 1/2% stomach, 1% enima or paps/douche(Put up feet raising ur hips up b4 bathroom for 5 sec max w down magnet. Lay there as long as possible. Rather take a bit less than go right away. Dr Ox is a power wash. Sometimes will have 2 go quick. Best to do b4 food so body can absorb it. Dr Hydro Ox is a powerful cleanser.), 1-2% skin(all over/can use an ear bulb). 2 1/2% gums(at least 5 min swish or tea tree oil). U can fully heal. Does more than any food can. No food can heal now. 99% is poi cause of spraying of the sky. Dr Ox rids Free radicals in brain even, helps gut health & all that. Is made in lab so is naturally fairly non toxic cause of the scientific process(xtra clean containers, exact ingredients, etc). Frankencense on Spine & brain am & pm protects nerves & Soul. Heals hurts quickly. Even ruptured nerves, ribs. Alcohol, aluminum, 24d, drugs... is bad. Lowers Spinal ener. Aluminum & 24d & other toxins r addictive drugs. 24d put me for yrs in anaphylactic shock/could not breathe, a small distance from death. Just from getting it on my hands. I would roll on the floor gasping for breath. Why eat poi that harms the Soul? Stay away from poi. Read labels. Test. 24d will put spots in ur sight. Dr Ox & Franken raise Spinal ener. Consider this from God/wants this info out. U can heal. Purity is necessary. Hydrogen & Oxygen r very powerful. R Holy. Get food grade from someone concerned w Pure 35% H2O2. After u make a gal of Dr Ox(Dr Hydro Ox), cover it w a dark grocery sac on bottom that tests ok tying it several inches belo lid to avoid facing the cap. Wen not using, put dark sac over the top too. Light will weaken it, especially sunlight will make it decompose. Squeeze a drop out of a bulb onto scalp. Instant relief from Free radical stiffness. Head vertebrea crack easier. Soak the scalp. Franken: MajesticPure or Radhabeauty & some others have it Pure & cheap(4 oz 15-$20. Can do volume or holiday deals w free shipping. But u still have to test to get a good batch. Remember it is easy for the s magnet to get into a batch cause of the 2012 ener shift. Dr Ox will k ill mold also. Industry uses this. Will clean ur insides. This world is purposely toxic. They want to make money. But the s magnet turns the Spine into a lot of different s shapes as it destroys the body from the toxic shortcut. Is the money worth it? Those w greed for money will lose everything & take us w them unless we fight very hard. Greed is neg lower ener that destroys by definition. All neg emotions destroy. But these 2 cures r the quickest way to fight. A shotgun. 99% of food is toxic now thanks to 80,000 toxins & especially bad oside air.. is painful not to have Pure healing Air from God. Holy powerful healing Air. Purity brings God & health. A biggie: Hot Drinks or food in paper or plastic is highest impurity. U r eating the plastic & paper w all the poi chemicals. This is also why u should not recycle. Recycle poi & u further ur coxxyx magnet. It is trash. Dont use a microwave unless u use glass. We need Pristine Purity.

All the scriptures of the world state we have to act human, not animalistic/in our lower neg centers, that we need Purity in all the forms. Vice is warned against, commandments established all over the world. By the time all is lived, we go thru many different countries. Even the Saints. Ramakrishna liberated Judas in the 1800s. Is liberated now. R we? Ramakrishna was one of the Wise men in Bible, was Rama, was Krishna, Babaji. The other Wise men were Sriyukteswar who is now El Morya & Lahari Mahasaya who has been many famous Saints. A Guru is a Wise man who can teach effectively the disciple. Has full control of Himself. Has full use of the 7th. So we learn in many bodies. Learn even tho if from a previous life very developed. Even if Final liberation. Then teach disciples. Shakespeare, a Final liberated Soul wanting to connect to like minds, went to study w John Dee, the Original 007. But these rules r to keep Purity, to keep from falling. Many even unadvanced remember past lives. Reincarnation was taken out of the Bible at the 2nd council of Constantinople, Turkey. The imp thing is not belief tho but actions. R they pos or neg ener producing, Pure or not? 2nd hand smoke & mirrors? I Purity 8 or i food ate? Food is poi these days.

The focus should b on Spir Eye, Spinal Heart or above head depending on the development. & focus is on pos emotions: Love the Joy in Spir Eye, Happy betw shoulderblades(Heart), feel Bliss above the head(7th/Saint).

Saints Love & adore each other w utmost respect as equals. But the Saints Love & adore 7th people here on Earth & treat Them w utmost respect as Their equal. R the boots on the ground fighting the evil ones. Lord Ashtar, Galactic commander of the fleet that is defending the populace, very much honored Me during a conference w Him. Did not expect that. Was amazing to Me the respect He shows Us boots on the ground. We, the boots on the ground, r fighting, r part of the Galactics to overpower evil/negativity not only in the material world but also from neg fallen beings in the Astral. Amebas. R help for the people of the Earth. Sometimes the founder of a religion may even embrace the dogma cause the people r so into it but They r not bound by it. Dogma will not give u safety. U have to walk ur talk.

This protection of Saints is in the oceans also. Many Dolphins & Whales r 7th even tho in a fish body. This is why the bad wanted to hunt & k i l l Them.

They in the higher Heavenly Realms have computer tech far beyond us. They can download a cosmic beam from the cosmic computer w HIGHLY POSITIVE HEALING Encodements onto a cd that does not weaken. Then the cd wen played can strengthen all the fings & Spinal magnet as much as possible. The person has to b Up to get such a cd. But then they can play it 24/7 to stay Up. I healed my family of serious conditions(stroke, etc) this way. This Ellegion cd is the only cd u will find that does not weaken. Computer/digital, even digital tv weakens. But the Ellegion cd strengthens all lifeforces in the body lifting a person to their top chakra plus 1.. as high as possible if the person was Up wen the tape was made. Same as being in my presence & just the opposite of bad sublinguals but much more powerful. An advancing technology. They can also read a person's past lives.

Some have Final liberation(Avatars & others can b pulled down in a crowd of down people to the Spir Eye/Medulla. Never belo the head). & some have been liberated for millions of years very close to Final liberation where the down ener usually never goes below the Spir Eye. Paramahansa Yogananda says Saints have their 7th for millions of yrs b4 They reach Final liberation & if They realized how far They had to go, They would stop b4 even starting. But all 7th have at the very least worked out most of Their karma not being able to fall below Heart. A big incentive for mortals to try to become a Saint in one lifetime. Must work hard. The reward is immunity to hell. They r Immortal. No more lower magnets below Heart. All this can b revealed thru testing if we wear the mask, fix all weakenings, put Spine in place adjusting w the knuckles going up & bending back away from weakenings & s people b4 testing, test long especially in the beginning, fast 1st then shop. Retest to improve accuracy wen u eat. Do right; follow Purity & Virtue. Have only pos emotions. Also to adjust neck, breathe in & hold jerking head side to side while hands r upturned, shoulder height fairly close to shoulders w elbows bent. There r other xrcises in the Stories book that help u keep a healthy Spine.

The test is how do we use the opportunities b4 us? We r given them from God. Do we use them to go forward or do we react w greed using the opportunity to advance the ego? R we ready to pass? Appreciate the opportunity b4 us? Or will we ignore the benefits that can b had? Never use them. Never receive the instant healings offered. Why not recognize & use the cure? Air heals..Pure Air. Where else can Up Saints heal u cept in upper Spine & u asking? Many talk bout the healing powers of Dr Ox & Up Saints, but action is required. Will we stick to our religious dogma or will we use the Company of God whose output is service to humanity? Use a sure thing that will bring success. Why never realize the opportunity being stuck in old ineffective beliefs? We need pos emotions & restraint from the painful road. 35% Dr Ox is about the only Pure around cause it is made in a lab. U take 2 Hydro & 2 Ox. That is it. They add an Ox to Pure distilled. Containers r cleaned well. They r concerned w accuracy, being scientists.

W testing we can look at pics & see each center to see as the Saints do where we r. Do I have neg magnets belo the Heart? R the lower centers locked in pos ener? Is this a clone I am looking at? A clone has no Soul & therefore no ener in any center. He also ages very quickly. Clones have to b redone often.

Wen u can test, u can buy a whole jar of appl sauce(fiber/ antioxidents) or a whole bunch of nanas(raw enzymes for digestion/nana has a very pos vibration) w one test. The poi is more concentrated in peel & seed of food so these r trash in today's world even tho they contain vitamins, etc. For instance the appl tree keeps the appl meat good for people. Eating enzyme pills for digestion will make the body dependant & not function properly. Will wreck digestion. Best to get enzymes from raw nanas(nana worms r part of the inside peel/ test medium bad/dont eat). Enzyme pills can b eaten on an empty stomach to clean problems in the body like a hurt ankle & other things if they test ok in the morning. Water may b necessary w the enzymes if it tests good. Enzymedica makes Enzyme Defense. Sunshine Naturals has pina-plus bromelain. I got a good batch of each. On a totally empty stomach, it can go into blood & clean it of undigested food treated as poi, lessen scars, etc. Helps Spinal magnet by getting rid of poi s. 45 min-1 hr later u can test Laminine which raises ener. 45 min-1 hr after Laminine tests can test food to see wen it tests ok. Could b longer. Is approx. Wen u test & wen u eat, test & eat in the least weakening place. Laminine, wen u find some that tests good, is good for the Soul. Is Holy like good Lecithin. Raises ener like Lecithin, Dr Ox & Franken. They r Pure Love. Dr Ox gives 100% concentration.

We generally go out wen the Air is good 2-3 hours a week. Sometimes 5. So we do not usually catch a cold but wen we do from accidental exposure at the store, we take Sambiscus Black Elderberry that we have had for a long time cause totally good non s organic Elderberry is hard to find & we hardly need it. We take only 4 oz of distilled water that day w the spoon of Elderberry. This is wat Paramahansa Yogananda taught.. to Dry out the nasal passages & the cold would b over in 24 hrs. This is the way the Yogis(r Saints/Gods) do it.

It is not good to overdo fat soluable vitamins. Too much A & E can really hurt the body. people have died from vitamin A overdose (polar bear liver). One can get a yellow growth over the white of the eye from too much betacarotine/carrot & green juice. S growths & other xtra in body turn worse s holding the Spinal magnet down causing inflammation & lack of Oxygen, just the opposite of why we Drink it. & in the head thoroughly wrecking our ener! E is found in the oil. Dont need much for antiaging. Moderation is the key. God knows best the amounts. They r very small in food.

Pills r not needed every day...the body usually keeps the good & gets rid of trash. Body is very intelligent & can even communicate if one knows how to read it like advanced Saints. Gelatin or vegie caps can b opened & contents poured in mouth. This limits possible s & eliminates gelatin & xtra plastic while helping absorption of the nutrients. But chew & swallow Laminine in the vegie caps. We supplemented w Yolks, fish oil, chia seeds & flax oil. Very occasionally would part of a Coq10, B12(dissolve under tongue so absorbed. is like shooting, older cannot utilize otherwise), D3, C(magnesium ascorbate) or B test good. Methyl Folate(a better form), B6. There were others. Dissolve under tongue b12, methyl folate and many more. Body can utilize better. Body needs b12 & other nutrients 2 function properly. Even helps getting in balance, aids Heart & the lil pancreas(lil fing), etc. We'd test del immune(good bacteria/not affect blood sugar like yogurt). We got most in our simple diet so we hardly needed any. Plenty of C in our citrus juice. No need to overdo & go down. Testing will prove this as all of this chap can b proven.

These days stalking up on food can b dangerous if one has an s magnet. Food can become s causing weakenings, becoming poi for the system. If one is Up, will still go to s, just less often. Same w clothes & other objects. Less is more. But we need to eat non s food.. buy more week to week. May go to s if too long at home so not good in this new age(2012 & on) to stalk up a lot even if on sale. Several weeks is max.

Soft ungrounded plastic in a metal fridge is very dangerous. Keep it grounded, compacted & out of the front door making sure it doesnt touch the metal sides or metal racks. Metal & plastic do not like each other. Will weaken worse if they touch. They have only one center active, the hate/enemy magnet.

Wen buying it is good to realize the next batch could b super bad. We have the spraying of the sky & wind to carry it everywhere. Even the country is polluted from the spraying of the sky, icides, hormones & the other toxins blown about for many miles. There is no organic compost anymore. Dont use fertilizer. Avoid even xtra leaves or anything xtra. Get them off ur garden. Is nothing organic. No area is safe in the world. Even the innermost South America(non NATO) is now reached by the spraying of the sky off the coast from positioned NATO aircraft carriers. I would do internet searches & find good things from stores on Amazon & Ebay(did many Ebay auctions), Vitacost, Piping Rock, Vitapal, Swanson & a host of others. Even got black seed oil from Isreal. They had a good batch wen noone else did. I tested products until I found a good one. Sometimes I would find nothing. 99% of the stuff tested bad. Same w finding good Spir Brass. I went thru 100s to find 1 usually.

I could eat honey so I bought a bunch of organic loaded w good nutrients back in the 1990s. To supplement the diet occasionally I found other good food at the grocery.. blackstrap molasses, sesame tahini... But internet searches enabled me to find a picture somewhere in the world where the batch was good. Then I would buy right away while they were selling that batch & I would b sent good testing items. Later I developed a way to get items Up helping others if they made a mistake.

I found some good testing Laminine - multi level lifepharmglobal.com - They eat this in the Heavens on occasion. They eat nothing else but God/Bliss of God being fully in the 7th. Ebay even sells it. It helps the Heart & raises the ener. The dark r afraid of it as they r of Rahn(Ra-N/vibration of the 7th/Halo w the miracles). They sing Rahn in the etheric Heavens. Since 2012 Rahn has a greater healing than Om/Amen/Amin. Rama is from Rahn. Ra & Ma. The Pa & Ma Rahn. Rahn technique raises Spinal ener cancelling the weakening outbreath. Rahn has a very good vibration u can test on ur fings. Is the highest state w the miracles. It raises Spinal ener wen u say it on outbreath if u r not down too bad. Say silent or loud if sleepy, etc. Is a powerful technique 2 deal w the new 2012 energies if 1 is not down too bad. Can do if we r up somewat. 24/7. Is known by various names: Only God 2 b gotten, illumination, nirbikalpa samadhi. They sing Rahn in the Heavens where Christ is ceo & there r many very advanced Creator Gods under Him as managers & supervisors.

Lecithin & Omega3 or egg Yolks, if u can find good testing, also raises the Spinal ener & is helpful to the Heart & brain. One yolk a day is vital if it tests ok. Egg white is the lubrication of the birth canal & acts like meat weakening all 5 lifeforces in body. & is a poi to the system by my testing. It is part of the chicken. They also spoil quickly out of the fridge but Yolks dont. I tested this on several. White gets stuck in the tissues & goes to s. Body has trouble eliminating it. Is mouse food. Takes u down.

But w brown organic eggs I have fond that the lighter ones on the whole test better than the darker brown. Same same w big vs smaller. Smaller meager ones sometimes seem to test better. One explanation is that they have more nutrients & therefore more poison. The chicken did not eat as meager perhaps.

These r some of the other things I found where the batch tested good:

B vit- Garden of Life Vitamin Code Raw B Complex

We ate no grain or beans yet could have a fraction of a pill a month at the most. We were Up & ate no sugar which needs b vitamins. Body holds on to nutrients. But people can b different & that is where testing comes in.

B6 & Methyl Folate(various tested ok)-test folate often

Multi vitamin- New Chapter

Black Strap Molasses-House of Herbs & others

Now Chlorella, Swanson Green Foods Broken Cell Wall Chlorella(green non metal will take metal out of body/had 1990 green pills but now w the spraying of the sky very hard to find good greens. About impossible.

Delimmune - Pure Research Products & Amazon, etc (acidolphus). No blood sugar problem like yogurt for neg magnet people.

Green Bee Propolis- from Natural Nectar(inflammation)

Tumeric(powerful for poisoning & high blood sugar) - Dont need Black Pepper. Most is s. Dont need much Tumeric

There is a tendancy to overdo food & nutrition. But it should not b overdone cause it is a Drug these days w a sex like effect: magnets in lowers leading to burnout/hell. Full control is necessary.

Coq10 I never needed any. My family took 1/4 or 1/8 very occasionally. More would weaken the body. Wen Up, body utilizes better so u need less. This is very common w supplements. Most people take too much of a supplement & thus weaken instead of helping the body defeating the purpose & wasting their money. Wen a person has a down magnet, pills wont b processed as well so there will b a greater need but most take too much. people also overmedicate on the food Drug. Testing will show exactly wat is needed.

Cause of the spraying of the sky, all vegies in supermarket now weaken off the scale. All r s. I dont even bother w them. Root vegies like potatoes, carrots, peanuts, most r just too toxic not being able to strain out poi. Rice is grown submerged so usually very toxic. Tumeric & tabioca at times I have found.

Purity's H A Joint Formula

100% Pure Black Seed oil(Piping Rock Cold Pressed & Solvent Free) very helpful for health. Spicy but best omega 6 u can get. One spoon. Has very high healing capacity. About the only omega 6 that we ate occasionally plus a bit seeds like soaked Chia. We stayed away from all the bad omega 6. Just Fish oil, Chia seeds, Sesame(protein) & Flax oil. The body has plenty fat w one Yolk, one Oil & one Chia a day. This is about all one can handle & not create a blood sugar problem or have excess weight which would cause magnets in the lower centers. ALL this was revealed to me thru testing.

For cancer we had Dr Ox; Coriolus PSP, a mushroom; Honopure(Econugenics/ Amazon); Graviola-went S(Therapeutic Labs/Amazon); Essaic tea(went S); Raspex

Rasberry seed powder-went S(smdi.org); Protocel-went S; green tea-went s. All these r good for cancer.

Problem w most teas, herbs & nuts.. they r s. Also beans & grains. If they arent, they will become s at the slightest influence of s objects or people. Plants r so close to the ground w s minerals & then all the s pest & other icides & s aluminum, etc. Forget peanuts, they r a root vegie. Vegetables, etc r known by the company they keep. Soil is toxic. Even trees many times cant filter out the poi.

Growing hydroponics.. no soil or metal w tested plant food, Dr ox instead of pumps, & filtered water (store metal filter blocking out emf w rubber) can help us avoid the ever increasing poi in food from the spraying of the sky, drugs(even prescrip), chemicals, icides, etc. Can also limit the s vibration wo soil. Can grow God food. Lil tomatoes, strawberries, watercress & others take very lil work. But we have to keep the house closed to poi air & s magnets.

Tea Tree oil or Oregonol/Oregono oil we bought under various labels to brush teeth, heal gums & breath. 5 min swish. Gets fungus on toes or any area. Inside full strength will rid parasites. A squirt of Franken on a cavity will get it much better over time. Sterilizes the rot, helps also the nerves to some extent. Rids imflammation.

Dr Ox anti-carcinogen/raises Spinal ener. Lack of will is a sign of lack of Oxygen caused by the aluminum & other poi in Air & neg magnets in Spine. Being wo Dr Ox freezes the mind to food or vice cause H_2O_2 DEPRIVATION LOWERS the MAGNET into the lower neg centers. It affects mood for that reason. coxxyx ener messes up the body's ability to utilize Air & liquid. Put Dr Ox all over. Spine, head, ears, face. Will keep face from aging so much. Keep skin taut. Also arms, legs, even underarms, everywhere cept in eyes or groin. Can carefully use around eyeball on skin. A small bulb can get Dr Ox on scalp very well squeezing a bit here & there directly onto scalp. Keeps u from spilling. Can Drip it down Spine, everywhere catching the Drops keeping it from Dripping off body disinfecting as we go. U will feel like a new person w excellant concentration. Liquid is absorbed readily. I have had a person tell me that their infected gums got better, their loose tooth stopped declining & tooth nerves from a fallen cavity got better from Dr Ox, tea tree oil & Franken in mouth. Will heal infections keeping gums from getting worse. Dr Ox after all gets rid of cancer, slime, pus & rot. When u dont brush, protect the teeth & gums by one of the oils at the least.

Food grade Hydrogen Peroxide(35% most Pure) can get from pureH2O2forhealth. com & others. It is the best anti-cancer cure cause it supplies Oxygen & Hydrogen directly in liquid form, both proven to nix cancer & easy to work w. Even nitrogen does. God knew wat He was doing creating Holy Air. Is why the dark ruin it. Dr Ox raises the Spinal ener & like a skilled surgeon cuts out cancer wo pain supplying the good cells w much needed Air sterilizing everything bringing health. Instant concentration for the mind thru bulb enima, scalp, head, nostrils. I bought gallons of the 35%. Is very cheap. Cures cancer anywhere & at any stage. The co2 in body is lessoned by Dr Ox which lessens the rat poison from barium in the spraying of the sky. 2 main ingredients of rat poison: barium combines readily w co2 whether in sky or body. We realize thru testing "I have to supply the deficient body w Ox, Hydro/Air." Body has a need to breathe.. Is not being met. Supply the Soul, keep Soul warm, ie Up in higher centers(the Soul is clothed w the body, after death w the Spinal blueprint). For Soul rinse underware.. Dr Ox bulb enima & bulb paps(douche) 1%. Put up ft while lying on back a few secs. & soaking the rest(1-2%).. putting all over body/soaking skin, walking in it on Crocs or ft in gallon bag. & a weak Dr Ox solution inside(1/4-½ %) if it tests. Always test. Comfortable. Rids bad bacteria caused by gmo, 24d & antibiotics, etc. Helps blood sugar & lifts us into a meditative/prayerful state. Fills us at mealtime cause it raises out of navel the ener. Gums 2½% Dr Ox. No stronger. Drug store hydrogen peroxide is too strong, is 3% & has added poi so not to Drink it. Very Oxygen deprived causes pain. Ox all over body helps immensely. Is like soaking in tub wo the face chemicals. Wakes up brain. Can think clearly. Hydro is also needed. Together they r much more powerful than Ox alone. Testing tells/diagonoses revealing the importance of all this. Dr Ox puts u in a state were the brain has ALL the MARBLES like a Saint. God made a scalpel that is practically free, Dr Ox. cuts out pus, slime & cancer healing the good cells instead of cutting, hurting. We need all our cells & organs. Is why God gave them to us. People use poisoned 3% on infections oside the body. So why not Pure inside where we need Dr Ox even more? & wo poison added. This s disease needs to be expunged & health reign. Is in Exodus & Eastern religions about health being a requirement for God sight. We r suffocating for lack of Air which alone causes all sickness. & Dr Ox helps to keep skin young, attached, tight. How could the skin or any organ function wo Air? Why do we demand that it does? God's will is to use Pure Air. But 1/4 Air & 3/4 POISON? Always resting, taking the easy way out, used Air puts u to sleep. That is the problem w used Air out here, u kno? We cant accomplish anything wo fuel, clean fuel.

Franken(anti-carcinogen) raises Spinal ener. Frankencense was brought for healing by the Wise cause it reverses cancer & all disease. Even helps pain & blood sugar. Raises Spinal ener bringing Oxygen in & rids inflammation. This is why it can heal ribs, torn nerves & pain, etc so quickly. The Spine & brain need Franken twice daily at least in today's environ if it tests. Will test if u limit other fat or increase xrcise. The nerve toxins hurt the nerves, brain & Spine. Can b used topically straight or if too strong, ½ & ½ w coconut or any oil on our hurt areas, Spine & brain. It will get inside from the skin. Can put on Heart area. Can b used inside ½ & ½ or full strength. In mouth probably full strength mixed w a lot of saliva-swish a lot b4 swallow. Full strength on cavities. We should test. There r not side effects like Drugs cause it reverses disease. It lifts the ener. Is not a Drug or poi that takes the ener down. But b sure to find Franken that has not been doused w poi & that is not s. Test well.

'Carcinogen I never thot of'- being down in neg centers as people r breathing the oside air, creates cancer. Also cheese stops u up, goes to s since it does not get eliminated easily Dropping the ener & it has too much fat. Who stops after one bite? Cheese is used extensively by the dark to destroy. Ox is not supplied very well by the Spine in the s. Is not working right. All is haywire. Even blood sugar even if u ate nothing. But u ate bad ener in the environ.. 3g, 4g, 5g, wifi, all emf. Is a long list of s frequencies that take ener to coxxyx, the mark of the beast. Beast or evil ones have neg destructive ener. Have to b in higher centers to b able to access the creative healing powers. Cant have ener in lowers; hurts the body & others around us for a great distance. Even if they just think of us. Is why in the paths people say a mantra like Rahn, a very powerful up vibration. Must test every bite. Chew well & swallow b4 testing next bite. Eat ur juice too. carbs(nana, appl sauce, juice) take close to 30 chews or swishes to mix w saliva so that digestion is proper. Indigestion causes blood poisoning. Test well juice & milk. Liquids conduct. Let it not b a bad frequency u r conducting. Down causes cancer, alz, ms, autism & the other nerve diseases. The definition of alz is the s magnet. Can weaken people 1/3 mi away. Down causes all diseases. Is the avoid zone.

For veins-Holistic Herbal Soluions(on Amazon) Grapeseed powder-went s. Threw it out. One has to remember the greatest nutrient is pos ener. This alone can make obsolete many of the nutrients. I can repeat, many times 1/8 pill strengthened & 1/4 weakened. But we were Up. The ener was more imp than the supplement. Throwing s out will protect our good food from going to s.

Omega 660 eggs or highest omega 3 u can find for the yolks. But organic pasture raised r better than cage Free. Less variables. Have to test well. No guessing. 12 tests. Some Coops or stores have a better selection & less s but we must test - pick & choose the non s. All 5 fings weaken w whites & meat. All 5 lifeforces. Heart, pancreas, digestion, everything. The body cant eliminate, digest, assimulate or metabolize them. Hurts the circulatory & respiratory currents. Ie, hurts the Heart. This is why Yogis dont eat meat.. keeps the Yogi Saint down practicing black. Fills the body w the neg emotions of the slaughtered animal. Just like the slaughtered baby in vax. You have to end an animal's life. Yogis take a vow not to hurt others cause it creates neg magnets in ourselves. Neg magnets hurt others very badly. Xtra stuff in body is sure to go to s wen we have neg magnets. Company/closeness is stronger than will.. does not take long. Bone broth is not necessary. Orange & grapefruit juice have pulp for collagen. But peels & seeds should not b eaten cause they retain too much poi 2 keep the fruit as Pure as possible.

We eat grapefruit & orange juice. Citrus has enuf vitamin C. Usually never had to take C unless we had appl juice which we occasionally had wen I could not find C juice. Hardly ever. Florida Natural, Tropicana & Simply Orange r non gmo but u still always have to test. Cartons try to avoid cause of possible leaching into the food. I can also find good Kroger & Meijers(no water added). We got pulp in our juice for the collagen. Water is not added to these so u dont have to deal w those toxins. There r other brands. Most is off the scale bad so u have to test very well & make sure ur next bite can b juice. Wen food is poured in a bad container, u can b sure it will also go to s. Recycling is toxic for our Spine. I dont recycle nor do I buy recycled products. Wen I find a good batch I test it all & bring home wat tests good. I skim 7 stars yogurt severely testing till I find no fat. The fat tests very bad. The fat mixes in from the trip from PA. Their nonfat is mixed w other farms & tests bad. I cant have milk cause of lactose. I eat the yogurt b4 buying so I kno I can have juice next. Unless u can test very well, it is better to not buy cartons. I avoid them & I can test well. I can see the ener. They can leach poi into the food. Dont bend them. Milk is better than yogurt & in fact yogurt weakens all 5 fings in people who have blood sugar problems or weight gain. So in ur system if u had milk so that juice is next, u should b able to test juice. Most should fast b4 shopping so they can test real well. So food will test like it is needed. Organic is necessary unless one can test real, real well(mostly Up). But some organic juice has added bad toxic water. The problem w whole fruit is they r very toxic. Test one good carton juice & u have the juice of many oranges. I can find orange juice but no oranges. I can find apple sauce but not apples(unsweetened motts, meijers, kroger, & others). Many times the organic in store tests bad. Am lucky to find any batch or even 1 jar of commercial or organic that test ok. So multiple stores & sales help. So for enzymes we eat a nana. Sometimes only half a nana. Test one bunch one time & u got a whole bunch. They r formed from the same one stem. The biggest nanas have the best chance to b good. Or the biggest bunch. The poison has more to poi so it will poi to a lesser degree. Nearly every week I can find 2 or 3 bunches either totally good or trace. Only on nanas & apple sauce organic is consistently worse than regular. But Dole is very toxic. Chiquita & others I seek to test. In all the years, I found only a few bunches of Dole. So if one finds the juice, nanas & apple sauce, they then need to find the milk but milk was the last thing they ate. I am able to test anyway cause I can see the ener of food very clearly. So I can even test commercial. But u may have to go buy & have a swallow or 2 of juice b4 u can find the organic milk. U can test & see if u had max potassium & magnesium in ur juice so that u know milk should test good next. Many times nanas or appl sauce dont test good until some juice has been taken w the milk so just test juice. So now ready for milk, can eliminate all bad milk easier. Wen proficient u can eliminate many bottles in a row wo looking away. U can test each in just a sec wen proficient cause the eyes build up an intolerance. After many jars ur eyes may burn so bad u have to look away for a break but testing in the beginning in the learning phase will b greatly speeded up wen one becomes proficient in this way. U will have to build up the intolerance again wen u go back to test but wont take long. In the beginning 5 minutes is necessary but later wen u find an item u think is good, u can tell in under a minute if it is really good.

At times I had to buy a can wen good food was scarce. We ate the solid but threw all liquid cause it soaked up metal. We usually did not buy cans nor did we eat the liquid food on aluminum.

At times I found 100% chocolate that tested good but it was very rare. 2-3 times in yrs. It also has fat which affects blood sugar & like cheese is not the most imp fat to eat.

Sugar & salt have no nutrition & can easily b hurtful to the body. White sugar needs b vitamins to digest. Brown sugar could easily affect the pancreas. All should b tested on the pancreas, the lil finger. Salt is an inorganic mineral that can easily cause water weight gain causing neg Spinal magnets. Will hold u down. There is plenty of sodium in milk, the only organic source of calcium.

Salt is very hard to get rid of. meanwhile it holds u down by the xtra liquid u retain usually in lower body. From gravity. even after a 10 day fast u can still have salt. People find their tissues still full of salt. So juice(potass), etc will be more even to the amount of milk(sodium). Testing will show wat u need. But if u have no salt buildup, u will need more milk than juice.

Incorporate this diet of juice, milk, appl, nana.... later will b more able 2 fast: 80% full. Once salt is out, more milk than juice will test 2 balance electrolytes. 2 to 1 in many cases. But that is wen salt is completely out.

Starch & all sugars/sweets cause cancer to flurish & should b avoided. There r cases where cancer was nearly gone in the bowel but just from 1 day starch, bleeding came back. Most starch has the enemys magnet. Imagine a big weight smash to the ground on xrcise equipment. We have to drop the xtra weight. It is toxic for the Soul.

If I eat for taste, that involves neg emotions.. 'More' consciousness. This is true even if we r moderate. Makes ener go down some which tells God, I dont want Ur Happiness. I dont care about Liberation. Or acting human. I want to act like an animal/lower neg ener. Or 'I want to put untested oil on my skin even tho it will make me go down. Dont want to age.' Body needs fat that helps Heart & brain. Tested fat for skin is ok if not vanity, a neg emotion. Dr Ox on skin will help keep skin young too. A bit Franken that tests could lessen inflammation while adding oil to skin. Wen everything is pointing toward destruction, this takes me down, that takes me down, one has to make an unpresedented effort to survive. But wen one feels ener going down from eating, it is too late. It means they should have quit at 80% full. Japanese politics. But quit. Change the scenery, brush teeth & go to bed & get closer to God away from weakenings. But fix weakenings as soon as u can figure out where they r. Get Up better on ur back. Neg ener goes down & Spir ener up. So sleeping on the floor now is bad cause of lowness & weakenings especially if a lower floor exists. Can happen any time. A top bunk bed 5 ft up would b great. In the pyramid(the square base grounds neg ener while Spir ener shoots out the tip to help the Earth ley lines or smaller pyramids to protect a home). Remember lower metal will weaken one less than higher up. But Japanese quit while stomach is a bit empty like true Yogis (Saints) do. That is why the Japs have better health. They r moderate. But those 4 oz or watever tested, they nourish every cell & can b totally digested never turning into undigested poi for the body to process. Body treats undigested as poison, not nutrition.

If renting & cant throw it out, wen laying down, face ur head toward the worst weakening like a big metal tv up high as in a hotel or a fridge. Motels mostly use oside air & many r just 1 story(vehicles will weaken). Get the highest floor available to escape as much neg ener as possible. Unplug ac & all u can. & ground metal on floor. Open plugs radiate electricity out 10 feet so is best not to stand in front. Quality Inn is a no. Way too much metal. Motel 6 has about the least. This can change but management at this time caters to that conclusion. Can block the metal, electricity & s w non s wood boards betw u & the weakening. If there r flourescents, see if they weaken less on or off. Dont leave metal in vicinity of a florescent. Will go to s.

Wat kind of chairs should we sit on? Non s non metal wooden where nailheads exposed r covered w 1/4" silicone or other similiar non s solution. Or plastic chair if tests for no outgassing. If tests ok, then no outgassing. So not to transmit bad Air frequencies such as wifi, phone, electricity, 5g, radio or any emf.

We should eat to feed the body by testing, not feed our whims. If we eat objects, r attached to food, that is a recipe for hell. Hopefully all our Loved ones will b safe. Think, is this food going to help the body? If it helps, eat. If it hurts or if the body does not appreciate it, dont. In time it will b habit. Always need to eat non s that tests good on fings to evolve or even to b Happy.

'Payment for all agreements-I failed on several fronts w food & I reaped the consequences. No God. The animal magnet is walking all over God's face & we cant see God. Happiness is not in vice but in the higher Spine, the only place where one feels the pos emotions. Where God is. 'Had I tested better...' Wen we mess up w food, the Saints cry for us. Our Saints cry for us cause we have a way out & r not taking it. They monitor us. We have to quit b4 it is too late. B4 we wreck the Spine, the Soul's blueprint & Home. The Spine does not rebuild itself after death. We cannot get Up if we die down like Immortals can. We have to rebuild. Is then usually a long process & a huge mistake.

Saints can talk to our bodies & They see what we do. They in the Etheric realm try to influence us to do right. This is where 'Oh b 1, can NO b'(1 in God saying no to bad/can say no) & 'ARE(reality) to Thee to' comes from. R2d2. We r robots & the Light & dark thots like radio waves guide/lead us for good or evil. Imagine following a purple orb & red orb. Which will we choose? We r Free right now. Let us take the Free. The

Free purpl path. For dark resistance, MAKE NOISE TO DROWN IT OUT w the path of Light.. do wat action God would take.

Following r the teachings of Paramahansa Yogananda. The currents in the fings r deliniated in 'How U Can Talk w God' & also there is some of it in the Paramahansa Yogananda Gita in 3 places. I expanded on that to bring it to us in this new post Mayan Eden becoming world.

It is a good thing to know how the food u eat will affect your body. Will it help the ener or hurt the ener of the body? I developed a means of doing this taking Paramahansa Yogananda's info in the Gita & How U Can Talk w God. In How U Can Talk w God Paramahansa Yogananda talks about the 5 life currents: elimination(thumb), circulatory(water/1ˢᵗ fing/Heart), digestion(middle fing/spoilage, mold, virus, bacteria), respiratory Air(4ᵗʰ fing/Heart, lungs, virus), metabolic(lil fing/pancreas, blood sugar, thyroid, bacteria, etc. One can test for mold(3,5), virus(3,4) & bacteria(3,5) on the 3 smallest fings. Wat a nice thing to know if food is spoiled or wat the problem is in ur body. All we have to do is learn to test.

One eats less, wen he eats per the testing to see wat the body needs & how body reacts to the food. It is a 100% science. But wen we eat like this we r very Happy & feel young like a teenager. Not so wen we eat food for food sake. I mean it is poison. How could we feel ok eating poi? Why would we put it in our mouth? But in this Pure state of testing every bite we can reach God & b w God cause we dont have the dark's impurity in the neg chakras blocking(braking) the way. It is a state of social security... of good karma, God cents. The best insurance u can buy to b in these pos emotions of the upper Spine. B in high school. If our nerves hurt it is a warning that we must change. Once we lose a chakra, all there is is a vacancy & we have to evolve back up... a big problem. Even w Spine healthy we could already have lost a chakra or 2. Keeping lifeforces in fings up & magnet up will protect u & keep u in God's Grace for a chance at evolving UP. Blood sugar is the single most used weapon by the dark to separate us from God/pos emotions. Calm is necessary of the body & mind. Coffee takes away calm. Is a weapon of the dark spinning electrons the wrong way. We think this life is real but Lord Ashtar(Ashtar Command in charge of millions of vehicles helping us mitigating some of the dark) said if we knew the Truth we could not handle it. That much effort is put in by the dark to keep this fake reality going right here on Earth. $4 billion a day. Remember we could have already lost a center wo Spinal problems.

Deformity comes at the very end. But even then choke the dark by right so u can live. All lifeforces need to b Up to help the magnet to b Up. Help the Spine.

To see how our lifeforces r affected by certain foods & certain amounts of foods, this is the way to learn to eat & is the best health insurance u can have. Test each bite to stay in balance w electrolytes. Keeping lifeforces strong will make it much easier to stay Up. If one is Up & keeps lifeforces in fings strong, one will NEVER get sick. So u have to hunt & pay for good Pure non s food that is scarce. U can tell wat ur Heart thinks of u & the effect on all the organs in the testing. Which organs need ur cooperation. The palm will tell you where your ener is if u dont feel it. There r ways u maybe can tell. Wen down it is not possible to get a good reading on testing. But u can tell if u r down by putting the palm in front of forehead for a good or bad result. If u put ur palm in front of ur forehead & it feels bad or worse than wo it or gives u a headache, that indicates u r down & need to focus on pos emotions to get Up. If u feel better then u r Up. If u dont know or r not sure, look at emotions & food intake for a clue. Try to get Up b4 u test.

An example of wat testing can do:

HI MICHAEL,

THE ENCODEMENTS ON THE CD I JUST GOT FROM YOU ARE EVEN MORE POWERFUL THAN THE TAPE I GOT FROM YOU 2½ YEARS AGO, WHICH HAD BEEN THE MOST STRENGTHENING THING I HAD EVER SEEN AT THAT TIME. I HAVE THE ABILITY TO SEE FREQUENCIES & THE ENERGY FLOWS FROM THE CHAKRAS. The 1st TAPE RESULTED IN A MIRACULOUS HEALING FOR MY MOM WHO WILL BE 98 SOON. SHE HAD A STROKE ABOUT 3 MONTHS b4 I GOT THAT FIRST TAPE & COULD NOT WALK AFTERWARD. I SAW THAT ALL OF HER ENERGY FLOWS WERE WEAK & GETTING WEAKER. SHE CONTINUED TO DECLINE FROM THAT TIME. WE SET UP A POTTY CHAIR NEXT TO HER BED, & THEN GOT A BEDPAN. NOW I KNOW THAT THOSE ENCODEMENTS WERE MEANT JUST FOR ME. BUT I NOTICED THAT WHEN THAT TAPE WAS PLAYING ALL OF HER ENERGY FLOWS WERE VERY STRONG FOR AS LONG AS THE TAPE WAS PLAYING. B4

THAT, I DID EVERYTHING I KNEW TO STRENGTHEN THEM, BUT THEY WOULD NOT STAY STRONG. SO WE PLAYED THE TAPE CONSTANTLY WHENEVER WE WERE AWAKE. SOON SHE WAS ABLE TO WALK AGAIN. JUST RECENTLY I NOTICED THAT THE ENERGY FLOW TO HER HEART WAS STARTING TO WEAKEN EVEN WHEN WE PLAYED THE TAPE. THIS NEW CD SEEMS TO KEEP IT STRONG.

NAMASTE, ~ WALT

Just like there r bad subliminals on tv ads, these are a progressing technology of Healing. Good very powerful encodements that RAISE the ENER not only TOTALLY UP but OPEN the NEXT CHAKRA/center.

W testing u can diagnose the elimination, circulatory, digestive, assimilative, respiratory, & metabolistic problems including cancer or any sickness. Poi or cancer, for instance, will hurt the elimination current long b4 it is a full blown disease. Can diagnose Heart, spoiled food, virus, bacterial infections, blood sugar, pain, allergies. Can see the effect of every bite on the body. That too much acts as a poison(allergy) weakening all 5 currents.

Ellegion said that the dark created coffee & mosquitoes to take us away from God. Coffee upsets God calm by messing up blood sugar. Mosquitos pester us.

One can verify good & bad sounds & their effect on the body. Very many sounds weaken: computer; cd sounds(except Ellegion that have those pos encodements); down people talking whether they r Saints, Healers or just people, especially s; many words: the word for a fallen d_____(ameba I will say/ has a better vibration)..., tearing paper.

Sounds that strengthen: Ocean; person who is Up; words Rahn(Ra-N), Walt, Mary, Freddie, Bill, Water, Donna, Carol...; running water in a brook, faucet or fountain; dvd(course the metal of the player will weaken & could go to s but the dvd frequency is good, the only electronic one). Rahn is the vibration of a fully Up 7th Saint. Saints sing Rahn in the Heavens. Since 2012 Rahn has a HIGHER vibration than Om/ Amen/Amin. If one does not go Up & down constantly & is somewat Up, they can use this technique 24/7. Repeating Rahn on the natural outbreath. At death we breathe out, a weakening effect which saying Rahn either in mind or verbal cancels the weakening. Brings ENER UP. Very powerful! Is how we advance. Unlike people who r stuck w the magnet they died w, Saints can go Up & down after death. Even the Final liberated ones like Christ, Krishna, Paramahansa Yogananda, Sriyukteswar, Lahari Mahasaya... They can b pulled down to the 6th which is very neg for Them & like the Ones wo Final who can get pulled down to the Heart, They will affect u giving u a coxxyx magnet wen They r 6th. So best unless one is sure by asking & verifying that a Saint died up, it is best not to think of Them. We cant trust our feelings for the Truth. This is why we did mantras like the Amen which is the Om. Rahn is where Rama comes from.. The Ra & the Ma united to b the invisible beyond creation in the Father. Melt into each other & dissappear like Star Trek. A Spir marriage, united which takes U 2 the Father.

Testing can isolate bad magnet objects & get rid of or neutralize them that can even weaken the metal eve which will carry to every room around the house(ie 'turned around an s mirror & set it against a wall. Tested it the next day. Was too bad to keep!'). Why hurt urself w s? Throw it out, put it in a plastic shed out back or something b4 it wrecks ur Spine & other objects. Get rid of the metal eve. This is post 2012. Metal transmits.

Cut out buttons & zippers, etc. Metal buttons & rivots on jeans, zipper weaken. Metal on centerline of body weakens even worse, even spraying of sky metal in body. Weakens worse than off centerline.

Earfones r k iller for the Spine for they turn shine into decline. No metal on head or centerline. Necklace, earrings, metal tatoos... Metal anywhere causes illness. Is not just from me but knowledgable Drs also. We need to buy jeans wo metal. There r some. Wear good testing sweats that fit but not skin tight. Lowers ener. Air metals from no mask can land up on our centerline weakening us constantly. & we transmit bad frequencies as if we were a cellfone. Plus amebas enter body wen we inhale poi. They r in poi. All metal & liquid in our body conducts these w a r frequencies. These days it is imp to ditch all metal whether food, jewelry, Air, electronics, poi metal tatoos(aluminum & more is in everything these days), every type. Wield the metal out of our environment like a great metal smith even largely the internet & fone. A dog does not have the ability to wear a mask & like the lightning bugs, squirrels & other animals will get senile from the spraying of the sky. I have seen bumble bees unable to avoid running into people, many lightning bugs too fearful to fly & squirrels very senile cause of this spraying. But we can & should protect ourselves from this. A mask(best possible that strains out most like Dr earloop mask) is necessary not to become a human transmitter of bad cell & other frequencies but also cover every inch cause the skin absorbs the poi. Then the emf magnify it. There is a Dr who has sensitivity to emf & talks about this. Another Dr warns about wearing metal. Car keys(but we dont need the weakening electronic capabilities/2006 & b4 cars avoid most of this/turn off wat u can on newer toxic cars). Credit cards(chip/mark of the beast), all magnetic strips & even bar codes weaken to various degrees & should b trashed along w labels on clothes, blankets, etc. Glossy paper is largely s as is foam. Glossy cardboard is many times s. Car keys & something for protection we need but most metal is not necessary for survival. Cars & other metal try to rubberize. Test to find the Truth. Has my cell gone to s? Do I protect myself from the aluminum & barium rat poi in the air?? Raw jet fuel? Do I eat the almond butter stuck on the aluminum top seal? Or pulp stuck on my juice inner aluminum seal? Or cheese wrapped in aluminum? It is trash.

Labels or tags on clothes r s. Elastic is s. Get high socks that protect from the spraying of the sky cutting 1/3 " belo the elastic to b sure u get it all. Pants wo metal many times have some elastic but a metal zipper would b much worse. So clothing labels, metal zippers, many papers, cords, much metal especially if exposed to corrupt emf of any kind, cardboard, much soft plastic & electronics mostly test bad. These weakenings have to b fixed or trashed otherwise u r 'eating' corrupt frequencies. They r affecting ur body even tho u havent eaten them. In essence u have. They take u down cutting off ur air supply.

If u have fone message files on ur computer & the people r s, will weaken computer & u cause it radiates bad frequencies. If bad enuf weakenings close to the computer, the computer will go to s weakening u till u ditch it for another or an Up Saint fixes the ener. Dont think of down people. U will inherit their magnet instantly. Can learn from people who r Up. This is why people do Mantras/repeat a highest vibration. Best to delete all down messages or down pictures so to give computer the best magnet possible.

W testing can realize long fasting results: 'Healing after struggling for months. Ridden of the acidic stiffness. Up better than ever in a long time.' In the beginning itchy toxins can come out in lumps especially if liquid has to b limited as w severe neg magnets.

The body isolates them in the skin getting ready to expel them wen given a chance. We must remember all toxins in body r already in liquid. Body is 80% liquid. It is this toxin liquid that needs to leave. Simple needs r resolved w testing-'Calcium I need, I thot last nite. & did not xrcise enuf... need to xrcise enuf today. Turns out calcium did not test good & I needed magnesium for the Heart instead. I still have plenty calcium. My reason had been wrong. The xrcise helped my fings.'

We have measuring spoons to test all. Test/measure every bite & get just the right amount for best health nutrition. For God nutrition. A sip, the smallest sip or a lil bite. It is imp to note that too big a bite especially toward the end of a meal could stress the system getting too much out of balance ending ur meal. But small bites u could keep at it extending the meal a long time.

These bring ener up. Length & intensity of Up or down magnet r wat determines the magnet:

Stand w feet apart w hands out 2 side shoulder height. Left palm up & right down.

Bend back w hands out 2 side shoulder height. Palms up.

Pos emotions

Double breathe ..even aides digestion. 2 in & 2 out. Make in breath a bit greater than out.

1 thing at a time

Calm. Cure diabetes swings by testing every bite & fixing every weakening.

Slow

Get centered on God after ea meal

The natural incoming Air is longer than outflowing breath. Wen in breath is longer than out breath, it takes ener up a bit. We breathe in at birth & out at death. So in brings Life toward the higher centers.

WHILE ON BACK put legs & feet up. Can raise hips off bed. Look at the prints. wen ur lifeforces start to weaken(eyes blink, burn or want to look away), put them back down. W down ener, will not b able to put up long. 5 (not longer) sec tho will get u up better. But must put down wen fings weaken so u dont get worse down. If just learning, limit the time since u cant test yet. Less blood in legs means less neg magnets. U can put them up again in a few minutes.

Spine doctored-2 see if Spinal vertebrea r in place, enuf Franken on for inflammation or if u put in ur back, u can check if u got it in/if ur done: test the Spine w fingerprints of one hand while u look at heart print of other hand. If enuf Franken, will test ok. Can test Spine at neck, lower back or anywhere.. If good till 21(about 42 sec) for instance, then u put on enuf Franken or got Spine in place.

1% Dr Ox paps(douche bulb) & bigger bulb enima. On back put up ur feet to bring Dr Ox in as far as possible for 5 sec till u feel a weakening effect. But not longer w neg magnets. Will raise ener. Dr Ox is a very skilled surgeon. Will foam up & clean our bodily house. Unparrelled cept for Frankencense. Dr Ox & Franken r a shotgun 2 raise Spinal ener 2 help 1 have their highest possible experience. 2xs a day. 1-2% all over head & body w a bulb keeping out of eyes. Soak the feet & Spine. Generous amounts on the brain w a bulb to get it on scalp while protecting the eyes. Keeps skin supplied w oxygen. Helps body 2 function.

Put Franken on Spine & brain protecting the Soul's Home at least twice daily if it tests ok. Limit fat intake more if it doesnt so it will. Put left, right & center head from front top all the way back to neck. Use for ur hurts & maybe Heart. H2O2 can b put on the skin but not in the eyeballs. Will help counter the spraying of the sky & also the effects of diabetes. The eyes need it & r not getting it. They burn wo. Eyelids & around. Will help eyes keeping them from burning so bad. Help them recover completely. Cover the eyes completely from the oside Air & look at scenery the least possible. U r looking at weakening poi. U can use just 1 eye & switch eyes giving each a break. Wear a high quality mask forming the metal strip over the nose. B a great metal smith weilding the metal out of the body. Join God w Delight instead of the various nervous, mad, hate & fright. The metal is very fine. Stays suspended in a room 12 hrs. Unimp? A Dr reporting at a live symposium even said if u want to b well, dont wear metal. Will act like an ANTENNA bringing in bad frequencies. Is also my conclusion from the testing. Dont wear spraying of the sky metal inside body. Will transmit emf. So cover every inch. Skin absorbs. Eyes will burn getting sick & u wont b able to tell if they r burning cause they r sick or the thing u r testing is bad. 1 person has this problem & tests w 1 eye only.

The testing shows the devastating effects of breathing in this metal or wearing metal. Many years ago I came to a place on I-40 in TX that had not even one radio station. I took out my Spir bangle & put it on to feel the ener. B4 all these bad frequencies in the Air like the 1800s, bangles helped but weaken terribly in wifi, fone, electricity, radio & all the other bad frequencies. My bangle did indeed lift me into a higher state cause there were no radio waves there in TX. This was b4 all the bad freq like 3,4,5g & wifi. So a good place to b is where no signals or tornados go like in a holler(God's freq avoids tornados, makes all better) if we can have neighbors to guard our house also. & no radio dishes or houses higher close by. Or underground. But dont wear bangles. B somewhere w in 30 miles of 4-5 big grocery stores w abundant, generous organic selections for shopping like Kroger. Metal shelves will make food worse so the least metal is best but in any store food might test good. The closer to metal the food is, the greater tendancy there is to get the s magnet from the emf transmitting metal. Once a disciple was testing jars & he held one in his hand while testing the others. They were all s. He then tested the one in his hand hopeing he had tested wrong but now it tested good. His pos ener had gotten the food Up so he was able to buy it. Much at store is freshly stocked so it is possible to find good on the metal shelves even way back. Some stores r frequented by s customers who take the things in store down too. So if everyone or many wear red leave, go to the next city or if u dont have other choices get Up best u can away from people & test real well cause like seeks out like. Can go to s easily especially around a lot of metal or s people. I went to 1 lumber store which had all wood on heavy metal. Not one board tested good. Emf took the metal to s which took all wood to s. Off the scale s. Have to test carefully & see. Growing hydroponics can go to s if we have a down magnet but the store is constantly refilled so it may have a better chance of not going to s as long as there r many good products & a minimun of metal shelves. But most have metal shelves. But even w metal shelves, we can find some. Once we r Up somewat, hydroponics r ideal on our xtra land away from house using Dr Ox, filtered water, tested plant food & non-metal tested tubs & building materials. Lay thick sheet rubber over ur hand filter. Test to see how much is needed to insulate it so u r not weakened. Cover exposed nails w 1/4 " silicone or calk. Most soil is full of aluminum or is s. Can we find soil to grow appl trees? We have the testing to set up the hydroponics. But no metal pumps. Dr Ox for Air. Away from house so wont weaken house. We need 3 acres at least so all can b at a safe distance. Human 'chicken coops' r created by the dark to destroy us. The Soul needs much more space.

Dr Ox cleans w a very powerful foam wo pain adding/giving Air to the starving healthy cells. Most Air is more poi than Air. Slowly take in wat is comfortable at one's own pace. 1/4-½% inside fixing the bad bacteria, deleting pus, cancer, blockages, pockets & disease. We have to clean up the mess, irrigate till we disinfect & destroy the mess inside. Delete the rats not wanted. Clean up infestation from any source weather slime in colon, pockets, cancer or watever. 2½% can heal gums along w Tea Tree oil or Oregonol. Also Franken for teeth & gums. If we test & it shows that the Heart does not need more liquid nor has too much liquid but still it complains w an occasional pain there, it may b a lack of Oxygen so test Dr Ox. Franken & Dr Ox on skin where the Heart is can give immediate relief. The Spine wen out from scoliosis & not bending back enuf does not supply Ox being down in the neg chakras. So there can b a shortage of Air from Spine in coxxyx or breathing in the spraying of the sky. One can feel the rush of ener/the tingling in the fings wen they r out to side shoulder height, palms up while bending back. Body needs 100% Air. Not less as Drs say is ok. God made Air 100% pure, not 25%. & we need 100% in our body not 96 or 98%. Body also needs pos ener. God's laws have to b lived. Less than 100% causes pain or the body to malfunction. Spread Dr Ox all over head & Spine (being careful of the eyes) so u dont pass out, then slowly bend back trying to hold as long as possible as many times as needed till u can feel ener coming thru to ur hands & hold longer. They will tingle. Arms need to b shoulder height out to the side w palms up. This alone helps to counter the neg flow. Try to bend back till ur head feels as low as ur waist. If u get dizzy is from being down too bad. Try to get Up better; check emotions & weakenings; & take it slow bending back. Once Up better the dizzyness will go away so just take it slow till u can get results from bending back. Then adjust Spine from bottom up careful not to press w the prints. Always go up. This aids the pos ener. Use knuckles which dont have neg ener. U can even use a defaced(explained later) piece of wood about 8" long so hands r 4" away from Spine. Bending back w palms upturned shoulder height stretched out to side straightens the back & is the only good way u can bend Spine cause it helps supply Air to body by straightening the Spine. It works the shoulders which are ignored by the down magnet person since there is no upper ener there. Bending back straightening Spinal problems caused by lower Spinal magnets lets the ener flow up bringing Air in naturally. This helps the Spinal magnet keeping neg palm interference away from the Spine therefore keeping one Up as much as possible. It also helps one to use the trunk not overworking legs & arms. Other Spinal adjustments do also which will b in the xrcise & nutrition section of the Stay Up stories book. The Dr Ropes.

41

To avoid:

Always keep a straight Spine never bending down as a baby does to pick up a toy on the floor or like touching the toes. Cuts Air flow to body/lowers Spinal ener. Bend knees. Bending back till head feels down by waist increases Air flow in Spine. To advance or become a Saint, one has to go to high school. Open & stabalize in each of the higher centers until the 7th is totally open for 3 years at which time one can stabalize there never to drop again to base of Spine. W Virtue, Purity & a straight Spine always we r ready to lift & keep the ener Up. Our foundation of the Soul's home, the Spine, is permanent. We have to commit to do right & take advantage of the benefits we can gain by right. Purity is needed. Poison has to b avoided. All vice equated frequencies avoid including metal conductance. God can be experienced by all.

Avoid bending the Spine like sleeping on the side or front. It is more imp, is critical to snore w a straight Spine on the back rather than to b on the stomach or side. The back must b braced. Spinal vertebrea have to stay in place. Hanging by arms can knock vertebrea out of place also. For anyone. Sleeping on side cuts the upward ener flow & lessens our pos magnets, devastating for our Spine, Soul & health which we cant afford in this post 2012 world. Some can get by longer than others but they cheat themselves of the greatest benefit they can witness.

S brass that used to conduct Spir ener is trash. Only a certain % of copper(87%) & tin(13%) make the Spir brass antenna. I did find 1 rare copper platter that was a Spir antenna. These antennas could b most any shape. Platter, lamp, horse. But the amount of Spir ener beamed from the Central Sun matters & can make good brass turn bad. This is wat happened to all our crystals. Cause of 2012 higher & higher ramp ups of ener I have not seen one good crystal in years unlike as in Atlantis wen they were heavily used. S Saints in the Heart cannot tell that a crystal tests bad. They cant feel all the ener in Spine. Down inhibits correct results. S crystals r trash.

S food- 'I dont eat s food.' Commercial is mostly no good. Many times 24d/roundup is used for harvest also which could affect non gmo. Non gmo has other icides from that yr or from earier crops, even 24d. Organic is best. Only has the spraying of the sky. 7 crops r gmo/24d. If it doesnt say on label organic, then it has roundup(24d) most likely at the very least on all gmo crops & most likely much more. There r other partial gmo crops besides bell peppers. All wheat, corn, soy, cotton, sugar beets, alphafa, pineapple r 24d/gmo as r some bell peppers. This wrecks our meat & milk products, sweets, pastries, breads, most. Is a fight to find something wo poison. Does the label have high fructose corn syrup, etc? Salt & sugar r poi too to the body. Comode waste is also used on plants that supply us w illegal prescription drugs & any of the 80,000 toxins found in life today. The root vegies found in most commercial food: potatoes, carrots, onions, garlic, beets, tabioca, etc, even rice which grows standing in water, r poisoned 5 or more ways w icides, the s magnet, spraying of the sky, drugs, etc. They cant strain them out. 'I dont eat roundup or other non gmo icides. I dont eat wat tests bad. I dont eat organic that tests for aluminum or other toxic substances. I dont eat root vegies or rice period'. Peanuts r a root vegie. Have u noticed the only non gmo in most convenience stores r root vegies or toxic vegies? Very occasionally I find tumeric. Tabioca I found b4 the mass poisoning but now cant find any.

'I eat very little fat & starch & definitely limit sugar & sweets.' Good blood sugar is the Holy grail of a Spiritually ready body that can b Calm, Happy & can advance. 'Wen I eat like this, I can get 3 times the work done. Helps me to b Up.'

Best way to have good hormones is to b Happy, Cheerful, Joyous(Love the joy), a Blissful refuge in God. Per a Dr: one stressful emotion messes up hormones 12 hrs & magnet also per my experience. Down wreaks havoc. Animal protein, even Organic, needs to b limited cause of the transient commercial hormones. They travel all over the animal spectrum. Do not stay in 1 place just like icides & all toxins that dont get washed down to rivers & then the Ocean. But bad hormones sho up in the testing if ur tests r accurate. Test carefully ur much needed Organic nonfat milk.

'I ask God & my higher self everything that I should do so I dont waste weeks in wrong.'

'I test metal & electronics to see the Truth of their effect on my body & the people & animals I Love around me. I dont eat s metal in food or in weakenings/environ. I trash it. I have replaced all metal in my mouth w a material that tests' (keep it in a Dental cubbord protected till he can put it in my mouth).

Weakenings - I need to fix weakenings especially in kitchen & bedroom where Im most of the time. But everywhere cause it affects me very seriously. & test food in the least weakening place so I get the best & most accurate results. Weakenings: tv, & the like will nix healings cause of the neg ener. Check ur phone. Phone is not worth ur Soul. Most weaken off the scale. If floor is weakening, things r affected the closer they r to the floor. A 1 story largely avoids this. Things r grounded better. Bad metal weakenings devastate our magnet. They need to b fixed. Metal is largely trash. The Spir Pro feels the s & gets rid of it b4 it takes other things to s or ruins Their Spinal magnet. Cannot test food if there r weakenings. Wont test good or will b an incorrect reading.

Cannot stay Up while sleeping if there r weakenings pulling us down. It is not wise to have metal in the bedroom. Playing even good radio will take u down cause of the s people. Most r s from the spraying of the sky. S weakenings & also s emf frequencies(dvd is only good 1) in the Air hit the metal radio pulling u down hurting all in ur house u pull down. Metal transmits. IF we r UP, we take others UP. Wen we go to sleep w a weakening, it will pull us further & further down. It takes us DOWN. Even if people talking on internet r not down as in an electronic weakening, the s metal transmitting interacts w Spir ener from Earth & neg emf magnifying the bad effect. A scientific fact. Creates a disastrous condition! We r down. Metal shelves acting as antennas, waves hitting washers, tv, fones, our bodies. Is no wonder. So much corruption transmitted. people r banning 5G cause of the k i l ling effect. There is a huge lawsuit cause of the damage it causes people but still they deploy it. For survival, weakenings have to b fixed.

A flag pole in the middle of the yard transmitting a weakening from across the street, will transmit it to the house. We should cut it down to protect our home. Wen the weakenings may b too bad, just do Dr Ox & lay down putting up feet briefly to get some relief. It will pull us up a bit. Face or point the head toward the worst weakening while laying down. This will give us max ability to counter the s. We will also b off the floor that is probably weakening. But fix all weakenings right away as soon as possible. Weakenings effect the Heart terribly.

Every rule God has is to avoid the consequences of the lower centers & avoid falling. We cant go to the different mansions or Heaven if we have lower magnets. Impossible. They pull us down to impurity which is possible hell. Since 2012, people r around the beamed Earth Spir ener. So it is even more imp to follow God's laws. If we do, we can advance very quickly, much quicker than b4 2012. But if we dont, we can go down much easier too. The Spir ener is toxic to a life of impurity. Can lose everything. Is God's test. He is not willing for us to continue in impurity. Is recycling the trash even if it is us in impurity just like in the time of Saints Sodom & Gomorrah. The ones that lost then still have not recovered. R history.

What makes one go down:

Breaking God's laws put there cause one will go down losing their Soul & health.

Metal cause of conducting all the bad frequencies will easily weaken/go to s. Also weaken things it touches. Like a metal lid. The food on the lid inside will go to s so it is wise to take it off of the lid wen u open the jar. Also dont lay down a full jar w a metal lid. All the food will go to s fairly quickly cause of touching the bad frequencies. Putting a huge package of chia on an s car will take chia to s.

Dont touch hands together. Weakens taking u down.

Wen u test b at least 1/2 ft above earth. Dont sit down on ground. Will take u down cause of the tug of wa r betw all the poison, metals & emf and pos God ener.

U want to b higher than weakenings. Ie not 1st floor on same level as cars or belo road where cars go by. Neg ener goes mostly down.

24d is a Drug, weakens taking u down & attacks the eyes. Is very hard to get rid of. puts floaters or spots in ur sight Weakenings in the head r especially bad. Aluminum & the other toxins r addictive too.

Pointing the 3 biggest fings toward Spine, front centerline(part of Spine) or toward the head. The thumb(elimination) correlates w the coxxyx, 1st fing(liquid/circulation) w the sacral & middle fing(digestion) w the navel. These r the neg centers in humans. Pointing the 3 fings toward Spine, front centerline or head will weaken the pos Spinal ener if the person has neg Spinal magnets in the lower centers. If a 7th person has magnets below the 7th, these will correspond to the 3 lower centers (Heart, Throat, Spir Eye) & again, the fings will weaken.

Touching or tensing the trunk weakens making us body conscious. Accomplished Saints have a relaxed stomach. This is a guide for us to succeed. All concentration should b on our upper chakra(Heart, Spir Eye, top head or above head depending on where we r stabalized) not on holding the stomach in thru tension. If we eat moderately/80% full, it will not stick out that much. But we need relaxation to experience the pos emotions. TENSION & STRETCHING takes ener down some. It is best to close off the 5 senses to advance. All 5 closed will open the sixth of intuition. It will create a powerful force to lift the ener so God can come to u. Can experience the true pos emotions. U wont want to use the phone or hear anything. It will seem like noise cause u have opened up to a Joy & Peace, maybe even Bliss beyond this world. The 3 neg centers r closed off. Try belly breathing at this stage & u will see that it is to b avoided unless u r having a baby delivered. Avoid the neg centers at all cost!

Wen on back laying down, if one has a down magnet, hands should not touch body. If u put up feet, lift arms off bed also otherwise the neg palms will pull the ener down. The palm radiates neg if there r lower magnets. While laying, palms up also unless one has a very good magnet. Palms duplicate the Spinal magnet. Helps us to stay Up better. The prints will weaken fairly quickly if one has neg magnets so dont put up feet a long time. The fings also weaken w neg Spinal magnets. This is why one should not eat wen down cause the digestive current is weak(middle fing). Indigestion supplies poi blood & not food or nutrition to the body. These laws can b verified thru testing. Also touching hands together, crossing legs, putting a foot bhind leg all weaken & should not b done.

Focusing on lower body weakens: 'My feet itch. I have to scratch.' Water weight falls to lower half of body from excess water, sodium & potassium. Creates neg magnets. Bending over for whatever reason doing work or not keeping Spine straight losing our Spinal composure drops ener. All concentration should b in our center of development. Focus on Spinal Heart if 4th, Spir Eye if 5th or 6th, or on or above the head for 7th(depnding on wat we experience).

Sweat, xtra hair & nails, & old scaly skin weaken from poi & r not needed. Need to get rid of wat u can. Other eliminations also at 1st sign. Why not trim the fat off our 'steak'? Eat only lean or pos ener on body or in environment.

Poison will give both u & who u want to poi the s magnet. Poi bugs? Why? Wen boric acid that tests will let u achieve ur goal? & save urself to boot. All drugs, toxins, weakenings, s people, the spraying of the sky, food for food sake, icides, alcohol & the like including the impurity of desire as in sex, all neg emotions(sad, hate, anger, fear, dread, boredom, mur der or overeating...) cause illness cause it causes the drop in Spinal ener. At w a r w oneself & God is a recipe for hell. Makes us go down. This is the w a r betw Light & dark. It is scientific, impurity causes a bad foundation to build upon & one falls again & again until the principles r honored & lived. One cannot have a house built on sand(impurity) & expect to flourish in God's pos emotions. One can only do so much wrong b4 he is punished by his Spine he created. But calmness is conducive to a Happy & Holy life. & is the key. Is found in Purity. Stabalize blood sugar for success in God, for success in Happiness. B in the upper centers.

The Saints in the afterlife r thin. This helps them to b Up. Wen the body has more fluid then necessary in the body as in salt or other retention, gravity forces the liquid down & therefore the ener to the lower neg chakras. Putting up feet helps 2 counter.

Toxins pull the ener down cause of their s impurity. They r naturally s. Inorganic minerals r naturally s. I did find some salt that was non s once from SaltWorks at seasalt.com. I used it to test for a sodium need(for balancing electrolytes). S has a profound BAD effect on the Spinal magnet. The perfect vibration as of a 7th Up Ellegion cd or a Saint all in their 7th can lift us all the way up banishing the lower magnets completely. Lift us to our stabalized chakra plus 1.. as far as we can go till we stabalize again. We r wat we 'eat'. Company w a perfect frequency is all we need. Then there is no lack of will. We have to learn to behave. S weakenings weigh on the Spine pulling the ener down. Breathing the spraying of the sky fills the body w metal & raw jet fuel. We go to s conducting emf by the metal & liquid in our bodies.

Lack of Franken in this new age to protect our brain & Spine from chemicals, nerve toxins, etc. These chemicals & toxins r nerve toxins cause nerves cant handle the mark of the beast/coxxyx ener. The nice thing about Franken, it kills inflammation, the main cause of disease, creating correct functioning, healing & Oxygen to come. Increases memory. Healing is very fast, even bruised, 1/2 broken ribs or a torn nerve. That is why there is instantly less pain. Franken does not have to cost an arm & a leg. A 4 oz bottle for $15-20 is a good price if it tests good(MajesticPure.com(volume order for less)). Radhabeauty.com & others may have even better deals but testing is key. '1 person was so stiff he could not even apply Franken for a day. After the 1st day of Franken his Spine got limp, normal & he could bend back.' Franken, the medicine of Kings & the Wise. Heals broken ribs & sprained wrist in days. Use on all things. Helps Heart. HELPS U GET UP. Loosens joints, helps ALL sickness, even kills cancer. No side effects. Can get too much but it will disperse. Hard to get too much topically. Test to see if u can have it then will never get too much. But limit unnecessary fat so Franken can test. Can even heal ur mouth somewat.

Lack of Dr Ox means a disease prone Spine... neg magnets. Dr Ox increases MEMORY. Drugs have side effects cause they cause the s magnet whether they r aluminum, icides, gmo, 24d, chemicals, fuel or any of the obvious drugs & alcohol. They k i l l.

Wat is in ur water? Is bath water filtered? The Berkey black filter filters out 99% or more of aluminum, 80% or more barium/rat poi & 99.9% or more fuel(raw jp8 jet fuel in spraying of the sky/Berkeyfilters.com 1-800-350-4170). But how can u keep it from going to s & taking ur house water pipe to s? Can not leave it connected. Must b disconnected & stored under a rubber sheet as far away & as low as possible but 1/2 ft above Earth.

Towel Dry very well/qtip dry inside ears/double breathe(2 in-2 out) in another room to get hot water chemicals out of ur lungs. Does the water catch on fire or smell? Food is full of drugs. Do we test? We have the ability by staying Up & testing to know which food or home material, even plastic or finding bpa, metal... wat is toxic & wat can heal. Always keep the spraying of the sky metal out of ur body & have only pos emotions. Even non s metal should be severely limited.

Wen showering, especially if one is avoiding water chemicals, metal filter(Can u rubberuize the filter? Problem is the pipe.) weakenings & taking showers once a week which is fine, it is best to soap & rinse ALL twice to get the toxic chemicals from food, etc off of us. The head(extention/most imp part of Spine), trunk(centerline both sides), feet & hands r affected more by poi. They transmit ener. They r the most imp to soap & should also b dried 1st. This will keep the magnet best possible. We get a discount on the price we pay to go toward God wen toxins r not on Spine, head, feet, hands & the rest does not reabsorb the toxic load. Like getting coupons. Have a clean non poi Spine, etc. Sweat, hair, nails & body oil weaken from all the toxins & ener. They should b least possible cutting hair & nails as short as possible. Cause of hot shower water releasing toxins, double breathe(2 in-2 out) far into the next room to get this out of ur lungs after u dried head, centerlines, feet & hands b4 finishing drying if u have been severely poisoned. Dry head & trunk extremely well but all well. Hands & feet very well. Dont let poi water Dry anywhere on body if uve been severely poisoned. All body parts r sensitive to poi, xtra oil, etc & weaken lifeforces if it does not test good. Even if u filter, unless u get it tested would b best to dry well. City water is not constant. At times could have bad chemicals that u missed & that ur filter cant pull out. & then ur hot water heater could have face inside, etc. Filters cant do the impossible like Saints. I am explaining how to b Pure. These matter much to our Soul & magnet; will matter to u after death wen u cant do anything about it. Towels need to be kept face Free. Hang on defaced non metal bar. Traces of face on body require u to wash the towels b4 too long. At times wash the wooden bar. Skin especially dry skin, the face is harder to get off. Cant use as hot & pores complicate the process.

Face(facecream toxic s chemicals & others that r s like fuel, roundup, makeup, a long list) can generally b gotten rid of by 5-6 washes in a defaced washer on the very hottest setting. Wen using a bucket to wash it is a bit simpler. These r explained further down. 5 soaps at the sink would get my hands totally good but I used a lot of soap testing each time the soap after lathering up vigoriously. Always test the soap, Will be more accurate unless u can see the frequency clearly/not have neg magnets. We need a lot of soap. Face is greasy. Mostly u can avoid hand washing now cause wearing gloves is more accepted. But if u get face chemicals on u from touching anything or outside air, u will have to wash to gain Purity.

Avoiding face, u will feel lighter, not suspended, more capable of doing something. It may heal u of a condition. This is how to escape these hellish chemicals which have the hell vibration & will give it to you. U can separate urself from face by wearing latex or similar gloves. Food is wrecked w face so u have to test. I picked the best foods to eat to avoid eating face while giving u full nutrition but u have to test. Non s wood or wool can b washed of face & you can put ur face free personals on that. Also rope can b washed for hanging but dont use metal clothes pins. Soft plastic will easily go to s. Remember to keep ur personals free of the toxic oside air. Ur bed needs to b face free also so u dont absorb bad or have a toxic load on ur Spine, head or centerline. Wherever u sit, cotton will absorb so u need to protect urself w clean plastic. If u wear something that does not absorb thru like wool or the artificial fabrics like polyester, synthetics, spandex, others; it will work except the face will b close to ur Spine & affect ur ener but it wont go into ur system so will b far better than cotton on the top layer if u do construction or the like. But at home best to wear defaced cotton. Algodon is (all God on)cotton in Spanish. The artificial mostly r s & they go 2 s quicker than God made cotton which lets the skin breathe. Tshirts of cotton right next to Spine tho will get affected easily by a down magnet & sweat which is full of the chemicals the body tries to eliminate. Body eliminates thru hair, nails, sweat & skin wat it cant elsewhere.

We need to remember, wen food is prepared, like crackers in a box or watever, since noone realizes fully about face, face is cooked in. But if u use ur own food, u can wash hot finishing w cold if it is not ABSORBANT as u do laundry. Never wash w hot a 1st need filter(1st Need by General Ecology 800 441 8166) also. Better to wash things like that in cold longer than to absorb the hot water chemicals & germs. Remember ur pot also. Face is everywhere: on ur table, everything that has been touched ever. Or not touched(raw or unburnt jet fuel). If u have a face free plate & face free spoon, dont set the spoon on the table. All open bags even slightly open that have face on oside cannot b trusted to reverse face free. The static will transfer face from oside the bag. But ones that r fully closed & faced on oside can b carefully & slowly opened wo touching inside & reversed for a face Free plastic to sit on or watever. Open the folds slowly. Remember the static will transfer so open slowly until u have all the top opening open & then bottom open partially, then reverse. Blow it thru remembering to breathe in again longer after u blow it thru to raise back up ur Spinal ener. If both sides are face free, is easy to reverse.

Detailed instructions on how u can wash clothes. All else is similar: Washing in a washer is similar to the bucket but u have to get washer defaced 1st which takes about 5 soap/rinse cycles. Use the highest water setting ALWAYS. & use the hottest setting possible. Wash the washer wo clothes so that water can splash up rinsing out the top face. Adding clothes 1st will not work as it will in a bucket. Can test the laundry suds to see if they r good on the 5th wash. Wen u put the clothes in, b carful not to touch the top. Fill clothes at most 2/3 full. 2 washes will get it usually to trace face. Maybe 3. 5 or more to totally good. Test the suds on the wash cycle, not the rinse. Cold water instead of hot & defacing skin as compared to a smooth surface take longer. Turn clothes inside out to make sure u get all face that will b next to ur skin & even the ones not next to your skin otherwise u dont get Purity but interference for your Spinal magnet from chemicals, toxic sweat, etc.

W the bucket fill clothes at most 2/3 full. Try to put faucet toward center of pail, not on side. Fill totally up w water overflowing on all sides & pour out completely 3 times while holding the clothes in submerged 2 get rid of the worst face. Pour out using ur baggie on ur hand to hold the clothes in. Then wash ur baggie. After 3 times submerged it is trace face so not so bad. After the 3rd time throw ur baggie that u held the clothes in w. U can start to use ur hand then being sure to rinse ur hand ea time unless u have been severely poisoned. If severely poisoned, get a new baggie.

On next 3 soap & rinses aggitate the clothes lifting them up & down getting also problem areas that u did not wash out b4 soaping. Each time wash/soap the top & top sides of the bucket above the water using a piece of laundry & a new baggie or your fings if u havent been severely poisoned. Each piece put on the newly defaced place until bucket is empty. Then pour out the rest of water, add the clothes & fill the bucket to overflowing rinsing all the clothes & the top of bucket putting them again on the defaced place. Will need to deface it. Ur hand & a bit higher too will need to b washed xtra each bucket full since it cant stand the hottest temp & is porous. For rinse, add the clothes 2 emoty bucket & water to overflowing on all sides. Pour out. On 3rd soap test the suds. Hopefully they r at most trace face. Each time soap the top & inside top of bucket, aggitate the clothes/lift several times. Also deface the place where u will set the laundry on the 2nd & 3rd soap. Set each piece that u washed on the defaced place to drain. On 3rd soap it should b trace good(totally good will need more soaps). Using cold water instead of hot will take longer & may need more soaps at end. See how good the bubbles r. Test long. Keep doing washes & rinses till laundry is as good as u want. Try not to touch the sides w the material as a precaution wen u take the clothes away from the bucket. Lift each item several times aggitating to clean it scrubbing the soiled areas w face free hand/s. Drip the least possible on the sides, carry fast across. I hold the item by the neck or waist, the highest part on body so face in case I messed up is as low as possible on body. This will help ur magnet b as good as possible. Rain will eventually clean a clothes line oside till more spraying of the sky. Wood does not absorb as much face & can b washed for a line inside w just hot water. Blankets if not soiled can b done in bucket wo soap. Each rinse wen getting soap out at end fill bucket below the last rinse but use as much water as possible. This will avoid old face from the last rinse. The hand & further up has to b washed even wen rinsing each time. Wen filling up the bucket, fill toward center. Dont let water run down the side of bucket. This will keep face out of ur clothes. Wen rinsing out the soap fill 1st time higher/highest. Wen u do the last rinse & the soap is out enuf, make sure water is lower in bucket than the last bucket. This will avoid traces of face on ur newly washed clothes. Sometimes u will get the soap out of 1 but the rest r too soapy. Pour out that water & fill anew. If u dripped on side of bucket taking a rinsed piece out, hang it up, then pour out the water filling next all the way up. Pour that out, then fill next time a lesser amount. Then u r ready to lift up & down getting soap out of the next piece, taking across edge quickly to hang up if soap is out.

Shower curtains r filthy w face. Many things r. Every time u touch the sink or tub, u get faced w those horrible chemicals. It is thruout the home taking things to s that it gets on. So again & again u wash w hot water 5-6 times. People can realize how chemicals spread if they think how rain & wind spread things. Is on everything ever touched till u clean it. It got much worse at the start of the spraying of the sky.

Honor the building blocks of life & we spiral up. We have to tune in w our higher Self cause the Saints, God's officers, work w our higher Self to reach us. They can 'talk' us if we try to help ourselves. Think thru us. That gives them the key. Otherwise their hands r tied. They can shine us, send us healing ener if we r not down too bad. They teach us in dreams. We cant listen to the dark & take the easy way out. It may hurt to give up desire at 1ˢᵗ but is much better if we do this in the long run. Get on God's wrong side & u will falter severely. Will bcome easy as we switch gears from desire to enjoying doing for God. Be M-T (empty) of desire like the story of the frogs saying M-T. Is such a great feeling to accomplish things! Is all sugar w God in our life. & our Heart will feel much better, b ok. We will wonder wat took us so long. Later if not do, hurt will b much worse facing the terrible ARE. Reality. Out of God's Grace in a punishment phase that lasts a very long time. The terrible reality where we realize God's laws r there to keep us safe in His Grace. R the actual building blocks of this reality. We punish ourselves by being weak. Is not allowed.

Marriage to food makes one go down. Eat even good, non s food that is too much & u go down. Allergic to too much. Ur fings all go to s at 1 point & then next goes ur magnet. Food is a drug these days. All the Drugs r found in our food now whether we r prescribed to them or not. Even nerve gas. Testing is vital so we know the quality of an item. Can't wash out or soak out the majority of poi. But if u eat, soak them for hrs in good water if possible to get some of the toxins out. & wash them w soap. Make sure the soaking water is ok but u can soap up w tap & get it off the surface. Dry it well. Drugs (even prescription) r composted on plants & trees from the toilet. & then there is the Air & all the rest of the toxic soup. Toxic marriage: food b4 God. No Happiness there. Only animalistic desires. Paramahansa Yogananda says food shouldnt eat u but look at all the broken Spines from too much. 'Food choked me, broke me & made me live in a dirty doghouse...in navel & below. A toxic soup of chemicals never fasting. Dont want muscular distrophy, alz, ms, autism...' Need a good Spine for a good afterlife. Ener does not just dissappear. This Spinal ener leaves w the Soul at death if 1 keeps the Heart center. Is the Soul's afterlife body.

Testing gives an out where one can say "I dont eat s; I dont eat fat cept very lil like a Yolk, omega 3 or olive oil, a bit seeds. I dont eat salt or sugar. It weakens terribly. One gains strength by seeing the bad effect on the body. Testing is a guide & great guidance/ strength to beat the predicament. To align ourselves w God, W goodness & the pos emotions. We can read the lifeforces. A complex machine this body is but we can analyse how to fix any health problems. Can READ the ENERGY EMMANATING out of the FINGERPRINTS. B on top of things.

W all the toxic frequencies, we see they r instrumental in establishing magnets in the neg chakras. But Dvds r a good frequency tho. Also cds made by Ellegion have a very good, high vibration if the person is Up who has requested the making of the cd. The Galactics who make the pos Encodements who r here to protect us from the dark have a wonderful growing technology of healing, lifting us to the highest center possible. Paramahansa Yogananda said They would come to help us & They r here helping all who call on Them. They r Saints.

"IN FACT, THE EFFECT THE PROLIFERATION OF CHEMICALS HAS HAD ON PEOPLE'S PHYSICAL & ASTRAL BODIES WAS NOT FACTORED IN ON THOSE WHO INCARNATED b4 ABOUT 1970. THIS WAS A DIRECTION THAT OUR SOCIETY DID NOT HAVE TO GO & SHOULD NOT HAVE GONE" From a Galactic Saint

6th or 6th w 7 open pretty much quit incarnating after 1970 cause of the danger from the proliferation of all the chemicals & other weakenings. It was just too dangerous.

It is totally scientific. You touch a pos wire to a neg one & they short out. By ingestion of poison we take pos upper ener into the neg lower centers & short out eventually. Let it not b ourself. Even if we med or pray we have to b aware of where the ener is & keep it only in the upper God centers.

There r only 2 paths, right & wrong. All religions talk bout the right & wrong way to do things. Do we listen to God's officers, the Saints who r Wise? Just like the bad witch who melted into a pool of nothingness wen she met the Good Witch, the pos Spir ener interacting w the s Spinal ener will eventually short out our Spinal centers. Takes away one by one our upper centers if we do bad enuf. So we cant run around driving a big Lincoln of a body..eat all this food that is very expensive to the well being of the Soul. Nor should we drive a Bug/small amounts of food but animal charateristics still. Dump trucks avoid. Why dump our bad magnet on others by giving into dark food. Is not loving God or people. 6th people r the most vulnerable to burnout of centers in

Spine cause theirs is a higher ener than 5th or 4th. 4th is the hardest to break. Is a less refined ener. But the s magnet even melted the wicked witch. W tv & electronics a new problem has been introduced cause we no longer honor 'Company is stronger than will power'. & we cant heal. Would we bring characters that talk about mu rder into our house to associate w our children? Would we bring s people into our home just cause they talk about virtue? Or would we rather get the cream of the crop to influence our children in our home? Ones we get a good feeling about. Do we honor scientific principles like the conductance of metal? Of liquid? Metal is everywhere & in us. Do we wear a mask? Or do we ignore common sense ignoring wat the company of these metals, liquid & bad frequencies do to us just cause everyone else is jumping off a cliff? 'I dont need help. Im good.' Even in the instructions of cell fones, the rfid warning states not to use around metal. Yet we use them in metal cars, around our metal filled body, metal phone, etc. Do we protect our good child tendancies so that they can grow up into adult right habits that operate on auto saving our will & effort? Fone is not worth our Soul. Even if we break down in the car, God & His Saints monitor us & will talk someone to help us.

The true & Wise path lifts the ener higher & higher until all is in the 7th & we r safe, stabalized & dont have to go out of our bodily home of God to b unprotected out of His presence, His Grace ever again. Go 'out no more' from the bodily home of God in the upper centers to the lowers. We can stay in His Grace in safety. This is true no matter wat our beliefs r, even if we dont believe, we still value the same moral codes as right. The bad, they tend to ignore facts believing wat they want... their desires but these r the ones who get punished by their actions.

I once met a bird whose master played an s tape (voice had an s magnet/was Spineless & was headed for hell). The Kakadu immediately drowned out the tape so severely nothing could b heard but the bird/was screaming louder than a big person. It was the most amazing thing. She felt the neg ener hurting her pulling her down to s & she fought for her life. The master had no choice but to turn the s person off. Instantly the bird was quiet.

Why follow an unsustainable lifestyle following vice & impurity? The s magnet radiates dark fear, anger & hate ener out of the coxxyx as if we had these qualities. K i l l ener. Just from eating drugged food or breathing drugged air. Aligned w the fallen, the red ener is from wrong actions. Why do people want to wear the colors red & black that hell is depicted in? Is depicted in these colors cause some have seen this Truth. Why not concentrate on pos ener. Light colors. This is our test. 2012 pos ener we must now b able to handle. Concentrate 2 save our Spine. Testing many things wears on ur magnet. Take a break from time to time to get up better. Test w 1 eye. If clothes r poi, depoi w good non poi paper towels ur top clothes along centerline of body or even ur prints on ur poi gloves. Will help u get up better. Clothes next to s clothes will go down temporarily but wen u remove the real bad 1, the others will recover. Saints work thru people. They want u to ask for help, use ur freewill & mean it w resistance of the dark. Cause of 2012 u will have 2 thro out s clothes & rebuy new non s. Is not a waste to trash s clothes trash. Is the only way to unite w God's frequency. If u r careful spending u will have the money. If u dont, the Saints will inspire someone to give u it. They monitor us. Every inch needs to b covered w the spraying of the sky. Shorts & short sleeves r toxic for Spine & Soul unless u r sure the Air is good. Neck needs to b covered/protected. These things matter to the Soul.

The fallen can hold people's minds for ransom. Nix their will by overpowering it keeping a person in s. Many can gang up & bully. All the while the s person thinks it is their fault, that they have to overcome. A dark overlay. Like deleting computer files but they show back up same place... cant delete wrong actions. Or trying to back up files that u r done w but cant. No habit solid enuf to work on autopilot. They mimic good sometimes trying to fool. But mostly work their unfulfilled desires on others thru control. They have lost their human status, lost their fingers. They dont have a Heart center anymore. The red coxxyx popped all their centers. R shorted out. They have nothing to lose & still insist on hopefully someone fulfilling some of their pesty desires that they cannot control or fulfill on their own.

If our role in life takes us down, it is unsustainable. We can do it for awhile but it is a downward spiral into oblivion. Why? Cause weakness hands over our body & Soul to the dark wo resistance from us. Why not get Up? Do we make noise to drown out those pesty insistances of weakness? Do we Say 'I want to succeed. This is not wat I want. I want to do right. I was set to do right'? Do we investigate where the thot is coming from? Or do we get bullied & beaten up by suggestions of weakness from the fallen we inhale w the toxic air, etc? Or inhale in toxic food we eat wo testing?

We can test our chakras & find out the true status of our Soul. How our Soul Spinal body really is. We can find out what will help & what will hurt us by testing. If something is really organic or not. 99% is bad in the store since 2012 & the spraying of the sky. So food cant heal like it used to. Can we pick out the 1%? R we willing to wear a mask that strains out the metal, etc? Is more imp than glasses. So that we can b Up & get good testing results? Not become extinct? Dr Ox & Franken can heal. Fasting will also raise the ener & is required to eliminate some of the poi. Dr Ox, Air is more imp than food. Air brings healing. Pure Air like Dr Ox. Lack of toxin ingestion is more imp than nutrition. S nutrition is not nutrition nor is poi nutrition nutrition. Rats die all the time from poi s nutrition. Or is it poi s candy that we & they eat? 'I dont eat s but food that has a good magnet that increases my pos Spinal ener magnet. Makes me more magnetic.' This is God cents. Common sense adapted to God, pos Spine. Is where healing, God & the miracles r. Finally out of hot water w God, we can have a good afterlife.

Testing is like reading the label, the Truth if we do it right no matter wat the label says. It is a science that will point out the Truth of the matter. Even if it is s. Chemicals & drugs r s by definition. Have side effects cause they have a low vibration/r hurtful. Many objects & frequencies r not wat we think & hurt us severely. Like metal jewelry(no necklace, earrings, earfones or any metal for health) especially metal on head or centerline. R antennas to hurt us. Why transmit kil ler emf on or in our body? Even tatoos w poison & metal. & food full of metal & poi. These things that give a coxxyx magnet r aborting the Soul over time. We have to b able to access the Soul. Can show our Love the most by doing all we can to undo this magnet. Not by wearing a ring. We have to adapt to these severe circumstances.

It is a time to do wo & if we'd test, we'd never take a bath unless we clean the tub many more times than we would think to. Face is in all public places & private homes, everywhere. We must consider the s magnet it gives. people must live Purity. The enemy vibration must b deleted.

Burning s outlawed. Burning s is not good to breathe or b around. Nana poi for wat reason? Face grease is very hard to get rid of. Is a time to touch thru gloves as the Drs do so the chemicals r not absorbed thru skin. Why would u want to poi lil bugs which poisons urself? Ur Spine? Why would u use poi to heat w? U will get the poi in u too. Will wreck ur magnet for possible hell.

We can take a shower standing on our plastic crocs. Is safe if enuf water has been run to get face out of the shower head. The perceived benefits of soaking in a tub can b gotten by putting Pure Dr Ox in low dilutions in a bag or on plastic shoes & then soak the body part. 1% will even fix ear infections in several days(fill ear 20 min, empty, Dry w qtip). Or spread all over body every day by hand or bulb. It is also cheaper & easier/ more productive than tub. Does not dry u out at 1-2%, in fact it keeps skin young cause skin gets Pure Air in water form which is moist & easy to apply. Does not hurt but helps Heart immensely. All that bath water weighs on the Heart. Is bad ener. Strains the Heart. Aluminum & other toxins in shower or bath water r absorbed into the skin. This adds to the toxic burden. One should dry very well & limit time exposure. Dry off the bad metals & other toxins. Dr Ox raises fings & magnet. No waste wen u apply or bad bath water, face chemicals, etc. Can relax then in bed & put up feet(helps magnet) instead of in a dirty face filled tub - all impurities & chlorine has to b filtered out. Is it filtered out? This is very hard to do. Testing gallons of distilled H2O, the best possibility, in the store will prove toxicity. Most bottled water is very toxic w impurities &/or not filled all the way(Air for bacteria to grow & then u have their poop/middle fing/ even has chemicals). For success buy distilled w no Air at top that tests. Keep level till home so least amount of Air in cap will prevent more bacterial toxins. Refrigerate till u make the Dr Ox for same reason. Do not drink purified or spring water. Is toxic, has bacteria & inorganic minerals that body rejects turning to s until they r eliminated. Also spraying of the sky. Even water made at home can b toxic & is most of the time. Did you wash, then test the equipment multiple times until all face was gone? The body will expel on its own wo a tub soak thru elimination & skin. Any benefit the tub could give is more than cancelled by the absorption of poi & the strain on Heart. How do u get face out of ur mouth? 2-3 soap swishes is the only way. It is not necessary & in fact harmful to Heart to soak in a tub. Will add to the wear. U cant just undo the wrong. Also wen we have a Heart problem or neg Spinal magnets(most people), soaking in a tub weakens the body the whole time. Weakened fings from all that water pull ener down making lifeforces even worse. Heart is next to all that water that it cannot have or handle. Whereas putting up ft a short time lifts ener & liquid. God common cents.

Wen we test & stay Up, we feel great. We dont ever need doctors usually unless we r a Saint & take on someone else's karma to help them grow. Wen Up, everything is going our way. We feel young, Cheerful & very Happy. At Peace, full of Love & Joy, Blissful.. The body in this state heals itself & the Saints can too. Wen we r down, the opposite happens. We r moving quickly toward destruction. Drugs always have side effects cause they pull the ener into the neg lower Spinal centers, the AVOID or WARNING zone.

Disease is caused by 2 things, lack of pos ener in the fings/lifeforces & lack of proper ener in the upper Spine(ie. neg lower Spinal ener) which radiates out the palms & arches. We must focus where we r for the ener to withdraw & go up. If a person is 4th, he can open only the 5th. Focus on Spinal Heart(betw shoulderblades). If a person is 5th, he can open only the 6th. Focus on Spir Eye(about betw eyebrows). If a person is 6th, he can open the 7th. Focus on Spir Eye(till open 7th). If in 6th concentrate on 6th. If 7th is open concentrate there. Focus then where the ener is. Ener is in the crown above the head but 1st it will b neg flat on the head, then pos flat on the head, & then it will b pos higher & higher above the head. They focus then on feeling the Bliss & go into the expansion expanding out into infinity in the Bliss. Saints w lower magnets in the Heart, throat & Spir Eye cannot access the expansion above the head but slightly. They must 1st raise the neg ener. Once pos flat on head, They can then access the Higher Chakras above head, not b4. It is not even possible for stabalized 7th people to have neg ener in the 3 lowest chakras. They radiate pos only. Their coxxyx is the Heart. That is as low as They can go & is for Them to b avoided. They r s there. Their voice weakens other people's, animal's, & plant's lifeforces. It hurts Their's also & Their nerves. We should not hurt others nor ourselves w our imperfections, impurities, false beliefs & desires even if we r Saints. We have to b responsible to how we affect others, especially mortals cause of their huge consequences(losing everything/hell). Testing all 7 chakras will show the state. But They r in God's main Grace/cannot fall to hell. 7th sacral = Throat; hurts them too but not as bad as s Heart. 7th lumbar = Spir Eye. They r bound somewat by food; hurts them. So They have only one place.. 7th above head(pos flat on head does not weaken either). Otherwise Their voice weakens, even neg flat on head & They r radiating neg overpowering & hurting others.

Advancement is a science. Preconceived ideas of how we can advance needs to b let go of for tested proven methods that work the 1st time. This is why the High Ones come. To show us the way. Trying to overcome does not work. It is a process of tuning in to the higher ener. It is a choice. The dark tells us that we will overcome cause they want us to fail. The dark would like us to think we have to overcome so we stay stuck in lack of Purity trying to overcome rather than avoid. Much easier to just avoid & b Pure automatically. Apply the opposite thot & action. Turn on the Light. Have all ener in the higher centers (our stabalized center or above)or if we r a Saint, have all ener above head(1000 petaled lotus). The dark would like us to think that we r not perfect or that we can adapt genetically to poi but God's law of Purity stands. Purity means no poi. Poi means impure. It is certainly not Pristine. Wen blown up poi vibrates as a hellish sound like the enemy sneaking. That is why the dark has impurity, to keep us down in the lower centers. That is why we still have backward poi added fossil fuel wen free ener is a go but is suppressed. Poi works for them. The fumes alone lower the magnet to s impurity whether smelling the raw fuel or the smoke. But God demands Purity. The Pure will see God. Pure in Heart means people r not in their neg centers. For Saints it means They r in their crown, not Their s Heart hurting others. We cannot have Love if we hurt others.

We must give away the s actions. Let them b charity to God for all He does for us. A symbol of our Love for Him & His pos emotions. So we can have pos emotions. After all the Saints have one job.. to help us fight against the dark to b in the uppers. In reality, all we have to do is avoid actions that keep us in our lowers replacing them w proven methods like avoidance of the things that make us go down. The biggest culpret? The spraying of the sky, then s frequencies, s metal & s electronics plus EATING, a big 1. Is a drug these days. We think listening to good data should help us overcome. It would if we had the Saint's Encodements being played that heal or Spiritually charged pos objects. But we overlook the dark's boobytrap of deadly s frequencies. You cannot salvage an s freq. It has to b trashed. Remember the story of the bird.

Two 7th people UP in 7th center COMPLETELY can lift a whole room full. Two who may not b totally Up in a room w 2 super s people that takes down the whole room will also take down the two 7th people. For example a 7th President in the beginning of His term w his two 7th Children lifted the whole audience so that the whole audience was Up. Later wen He was alone & the Children were not there(1 had Final liberation), He could not keep the audience Up & in fact the s people who were not pulled Up, who were too bad to get pulled Up, pulled everyone down including the President Himself temporarily. Like a 7th magnet where ALL is in the 7th, a coxxyx magnet is very powerful in a neg way. All is s. Like a wicked witch it destroys. All the ener is in just one chakra. One s person can pull down a huge amount of people. Had the Children been there, most in the huge auditorium would have been Up except the ones who were too bad to get Up & they would have gotten worse not being able to handle Spir ener. If there were too many severe S, they could even overcome three 7th people.

This also happens w objects like metal that is very s. A tug of w ar. Which ener will dominate? Or frequencies that hit objects. Some can b transmuted or grounded but most cannot. If we guard against these neg expressions, we can stay Up much better. They wont b pulling us down.

We have to stay Up in our higher center that we stabalized in opening the next & keeping it open to advance to the next chakra. Since 2012, it takes 3 years. Except 4th advancing to 5th, not as imp there to b always Up w the 5th open but keeping the ener in 4th & 5th will pull it out of the neg chakras which slow down advancement. Generally we need to keep lifeforces...the fings good to get Up good. It is powerful protection to have both the fings(lifeforces in the prints of fings & toes) & magnet Up. Our testing will b super then!

Wat happens wen we eat or drink too much is all 5 fings will weaken like a POISON. The body cant digest that much & the xtra food actually becomes poi in body. Body treats undigested food as poi. Ie, we r allergic to too much food. Eating xtra? might as well b smoking. Is poi for body & achieves same result.. the s Spinal magnet. It helps very much to squeeze out the cloth(body) after 4pm...fast wo liquid. Purpose is to get Up better. A Dry body keeps from transmitting or conducting the bad frequencies that r around & in us as much. It is a simple but miraculous way for an s person to bypass the destructive powers of the downward s. Needs liquid to conduct. This gives the s person a chance to get Up better via Dr Ox, Franken, bending back, adjusting Spine & dancing as They do in Heaven keeping Spine straight w hips inline. Proper xrcise increases circulation, is powerful to reverse the magnet & will b deeply discussed in the Dr Ropes & other stories of the story book. The Saints dont move Their hips. They realize it weakens cause it moves Their ener downward. They'd feel it. Proper xrcise raises the Spinal ener so we can comfortably & safely sleep in our high bunk 5 ft up avoiding many possible weakenings that can happen while we sleep. Wen we feel we just cant dance or bend back, adjust Spine, just keep moving anyway. Movement, xrcise will get ener out of Spine so it can raise. Movement is like constantly changing/ updating the Soul's clothes to dress the Soul the best possible.

Freddy

Freddy the rat lived in a broken down fridge in the old part of the house. Freddy was easy going but never had any Peace. How could he stabalize blood sugar for God calmness wen all was poi? How 2 b Pure in an impure world? After all he was very weak. The Saints warned him a metal fridge would make him xtra hungry cause of the metal conducting the giant's yfly in the air. Why should we fly? Cause God said so. Freddy wanted to take a lease of Love but a yr commitment he didnt quite kno how 2 do. He could not find his hunger cutoff switch.

Saint Goldenbeard, giver of Courage & destroyer of fear, said 2 Freddy 'test the thot coming in since u have 1 thing u know bout the thinker. Was it good or from the giants or fallen amebas? Goldenbeard added 'The metal & liquid in ur legs will conduct yflys burning up ur Heart & brain. Why not test ur thumb to see the piling up of addictive drugs u inhale? The drugs & yflys will fry ur brain, Spine & nerves. Fry all systems. They k ill the famous & get by w it. Dont u think they can k ill an unknown like u? Just test the thot on ur fings to see where it is coming from. Worse thumb or elimination means selling out to an ameba's desire. Why put the poison food in ur mouth? Another step toward hell? Is the enemy vibration. U can tell by testing. Saint thots would make thumb better or stay the same. Goldenbeard continued 'Hydrogen & Oxygen purifies the magnet for They r Holy. Rather dance than eating foodstuff, xrcising the straight Spine. & bending back to counter the poi. Wen dancing, remember to move the neck up right, down center, up left. Keep going to keep the neck healthy doing the Rahn(r_ah-N) dance. Bend the knees while the hands go up all the way over ur head w eyes following while still doing the neck. Then straighten legs while bring hands & sight to hands at chest. Start at 1 side going up & down over & over moving each time a lil closer 2 the other side. In the very beginning u will b lower in stance w more repetitions going side 2 side. maybe 5. Gradually ull get further up so that at end of dance u r up highest & do only left-right.. only 2 going side2side. This makes a powerful circulation. If u test ur Heart circulation pointing fing, ud not want to eat that wrong. Does it strengthen or weaken the Heart lifeforce? Always check.

Freddie did the Rahn dance but wasnt consistant.

Saint Mukti done w a successful mission dying UP on Her way to Heaven decided to pay Freddy a visit. Caught him eating; said r u eating again? Operate on the lil pancreas for success. Test ur pan, the lil fing. Operating the pan testing u r sure to win the battle. Can see the effect of the foodstuff so u wont eat. Dont b like the woman who lived in the giant's shoe in bottom Spine. Had so many new kid tendancies she didnt kno wat 2 do. Test where the tendancy or thot is coming from. Freddy tested his thots his mind picked up like a radio but did not understand about control, strength & all the vice equated poi & yflys. He thot 'Well, all evil is glorified. How could everyone b wrong? How could anyone b perfect?'

He did not have to lock the house cause it did not have a door. Freddy enjoyed having rat guests being the host of the party & in private he'd find some rat poi & inhaled it quickly ignoring common cents, the kind that made good God money karma in his Spine. Purity. Being weak, he did not trouble himself w details. After all, he did not put out the rat poison. He understood about the 2nd hand smoke & mirrors. But was it possible to escape death & tricks? He did not want to worry & wanted other rats to like him so his philosophy was just to not think, to ignore the Truth glaring at him. How could he control? He ate so much free rat poi foodstuff that he could not think very well. Freddy realized metal conducted but discounted it along w the metal & liquid in his gravity filled legs. He figured he was still alive. How could he b strong? & u have to die of something. The Saints warned him bout keeping company w the enemy's sky poi & yfly. That he wouldnt fly to a good place in the afterlife hanging w the hellers in life. But hell was the only option cause the Spinal ener bcame too heavy from eating the vice equated poi. & he certainly could not fly in Joy.

God tested all the rats beaming Spir ener from His central Sun of the universe to our Sun & then stepped down again to Earth. Would they do right & fight or would they ignore & take the easy way failing the test? Swim or bow out like the wicked witch wen she met the Good 'of God' Witch. Melt into nothingness.

One day Freddy was under the weather hiding in his little house fridge sick of a dose of rat poison he inhaled. A ghost came by who had fallen & said to him "Twix, twix the terrible ARE". The terrible reality, the Truth that we must live by God's laws to avoid hell. The heavy neg sinking Spinal ener brings hell if long enuf in it. If we misbehave, we r attracted to that level where the others r who also misbehaved/the lower regions after death where we lose the ability to eat...all the vice people. The human vehicle is much desired by all but who takes care to keep it? Well, Freddy had for years inhaled but now had taken his last rat poi & was on his death bed headed for hell. The Saints could not help him anymore. They had tried all his life to help him but he ignored them. Could not fight the suggestions of the dark & wrecked his Spine. 'Ate' the yfly too. Humpty dumpty magnet sat on the wall too long not choosing a side. Dumptruck magnet he dumped on all who came around finally imploded from his big belly. No more Spinal blueprint for the Soul. God's Kings lost him. Was beyond repair.

Moral: Have to decide which side to b on. B inside the house of God w key guarded & door locked in the pos emotions of the upper Spine where there is only Life, not sickness. Dont hide the key in grass or under a rock. Keep it away from the animals. Then after high school passing all the tests for being human we can get our college degree w the help of a Sainta at the north pole of our Spine. Being then Immortal Saints immune from hell Free forever from most ill. Never surrender to the weak tendancies. why fear leaving foodstuff bhind? Is not even food. Might as well fight & conquer, have Courage keeping the human Spinal blueprint the Soul has to have. Just adopt new activities. Get Pure food in the right time, wen it tests. If we keep company w all our rat tendencies, we never can enJoy the Joy or feel the Bliss of the Holy life. Or Happy, Cheerful. We give up wo a fight. Quit b4 we start. We must fight to gain Peace that is in the perfect life or the giants get a home run separating out our Soul for the k i l l. For a trophe. He who inhales rat poison deserves to die/become extinct. R we wearing a mask or inhaling rat poison & other deadly foodstuff? Looks like food but is recycled trash & spit. It is not enuf that things r getting better. We still could die & go to hell cause we ignored Purity. Drop ego all at once. Lower neg magnets is the definition of impurity exposing us to a hellish afterlife if we dont live long enuf to recover. Purity is continence in everything. Is avoidance of s ener.

Freddie has to recreate his astral body destroyed by neglect of the laws so he is punished. Wen we claim a chakra, ie stabalize on 1, we should not slack off & develop neg magnets in the lower neg centers. The human vehicle is a special creation. The human has the ability to Love & has 5 fings. Fings open a door most animals dont have. A human can Love cause he has stabalized(Heart center open) on his Heart center at least. Happy only exists in the Heart or above. The Saints in the Angelic realm have 6 fings. Animals usually have none & unless they have their Heart center open, cannot feel Happiness. The more advanced guerrilla has fings. Minerals cant Love nor do they move. Jars dont like to touch. They have less Love than plants & they will weaken worse if u touch 2 s jars together. I could see this by seeing the ener flows get worse. It shows up on testing. But wood & paper from plants u can put metal in wo it weakening worse. Minerals exist for billions of years to evolve to the highest mineral metal, gold. Plants still cant move w feet much less have hands. They dont eat. A plant is as far from human as a human is from a God/a Saint. A tree is higher than a small plant. Animals eat but most dont have the Heart open. They can b quite viscious & force themselves on others of their species. Pets & some others have a partial Heart. They have the ability to develop all their Heart.

Wat better way to serve or med than to have pos magnets so we dont hurt others nor ourselves. This is our dharma that we vowed to do after all. Our duty. It is the base of all religions whether new age or any other. Not hurt, have Purity, etc. Only Love. & proper xrcise so that the Spine & body can heal as I will explain is necessary for non injury to ourself & others.

One has to keep a straight Spine 24/7 even wen bending down to pick something up. I sleep on my back. I put in my back b4 & after sleep & b4 med. Babies bend over at their waist to pick up a toy off the floor by their feet but the Spir adult who has been thru high school(in the higher centers) knows that a straight Spine is key to keeping hours of hard work from evaporating in an instant. Sit, dont bend over, if u wash clothes by hand or any other 'toy' that has our attention. Keep the Spine straight. Also CHEERFUL has a REAL GOOD vibration like Bliss for those who cant feel Bliss. If our Spine is starting to bend, we need to bend back to stop it. So we can access the pos emotions. This is extremely imp. To b Happy & Cheerful conscious of the Heart Spinal center, or Love the Joy at Spir Eye, or feel Bliss flat on or above the head or expanding to infinity.

Best to not concentrate on feet, legs or lower body. It makes u go down. It also takes the concentration away from your upper centers that you want to develop.

Wen I finish putting in place my Spine for med w xrcise from Paramahansa Yogananda & xrcise I developed, my palms r upward, about shoulder height & away from my upper body. My elbows r bent & wrist bent also a bit.

I put in my back b4 & after laying down. B4 to get the best sleep w a straight Spine. After to have max Spinal straightness in activity. I adjust the Spine w walking from Paramahansa Yogananda, neck side to side that I created & do w my breath held. Also a side to side for the lower back & a few others. I will give details later in the Dr Ropes story of the Story book. Wo this Spinal adjustment the Spine is not as functional as possible. The purpose of a straight Spine is so ener can move up. Adjusting allows for an enhanced straight Spine.

We need to say to God 'I give u my food & my sleep to stay alive' if we must. & we must. God constantly serves us. Very imp: Purity - keep poi Air & other poi out of body. If we move away from God by weakenings, God sees it as an enhanced moving violation if we go to s. & so we pay thru health & other means. Pay a huge fine. A big electric bill in our Soul house that is smouldering. We pay w our nerves & Spine. Testing is key to turning this around & EVERYONE has the ABILITY.

Because of the 2012 Spir energies, cause of the sheer volume of neg magnets including the fallen amebas interacting w Spir ener; it is easier to succeed but also easier to fail. It is a very bad MASS karma. Dissolution. A punishment, a mass extinction for this time has been warned about by Saints all over the world. Even the Mayans were told of this particular time. Their calandar ended in 2012. Would next b a new beginning. Will we make this a new beginning or is it our end? We each have to decide but we cant continue in the same patterns & succeed. Is happening. Will we dodge the bullet or grow the Soul?

For help to hold on & stay Up: Dr Ox & Franken. Putting up feet briefly, fixing weakenings. These r only a few but extremely imp ones. Wen our skin is grayish in spots or we have brain fog, there is a very great need for Dr Ox, Franken & fasting.

We dont have the ability to control our thots but we do have control over our emotions if we choose 2. We can always react w Love & Joy. Just one desire. To please God. 4th people can feel Cheerfulness, the closest thing for them to Bliss. In the 5th chakra one can feel Peace but focus on Loving the Joy at the Spir Eye. 6th chakra people should focus on Loving the Joy at the Spir Eye. Many times they tense betw the eyebrows if they r in 6th. Wen the 1000 petaled lotus is opened, one experiences Bliss in a greater & greater way. Ener can b neg flat on head, later pos flat on the head, still later the expansion beginning w 1st the ener rising above the head & later expanding to infinity. God is in every speck of creation. One can see the Formless Spirit covering a whole field as far as the eyes can see. Is scintillating.

Wen we r in the lowers, the Soul is dangerously living oside its Home of the Upper centers w God & can die a hellish death. Should not have magnets in lower centers. Wen we live w the pleasures of this world, we r rejecting the goodness of Life, of God. We take in poi & expect to b Happy. We have to b in the world but not of it. B in the pos emotions, God's reality. Not here to experience the 5 senses but close them off & open the 6th sense: Intuition. We do this by helping others & following the road of the Saints. Is service to the less fortunate to save them from dire hardship especially after death. This includes ourselves. Serve our good tendancies.

Normally Spinal ener goes one way, up. people in vice or impurity if long enuf there find themselves stuck in the lower states & cant even experience the higher God-like states anymore. Spiritually blinded they cant feel Bliss or have Spir experiences/the pos emotions. They have trouble moving the Spinal ener up. Have many times lost that ability to find they have a 2 way highway where the ener can go down easier than up. A broken Spine like Freddie. The Saints could not help him. U have to make 900 CALLs then to God instead of 800 Free CALLs. The wires to God r cut/nerves damaged. U HAVE TO PAY, PAY, PAY & GET VERY LIL. For results u have to eat like a bird cause u r in trouble. Spine is broken.. u r acting like a hungry animal. Cant let the animal wreck our perception of God. We have to b w God. God reminding activities, not vice. W food, we dont renounce it. We just wait till it tests.

This is a time of God's dissolution. Is the end of 4 cycles. One is the 26000 yr cycle covering the different ages. The 4th cycle has never happened b4. We r in uncharted territory w 2012. Have to Fast & Pray/Med. Religion does not matter but Virtue does. Living good avoiding bad matters. We cant look back at restaurants, anger, or whatever vice. Or even necessary food. It has to test good. Cant steal food. Will fall to hell. Or now eating emf beams or I am oblivious to breathing the oside air. I'm good. It does not matter wat vice or impurity we choose or is forced on us. Wat matters is to abolish that impurity & b in conscious contact of God. In Heart or above. All neg emotions even greed for food will take us to a hellish torture. The spraying of the sky will take us there. Any impurity will take us there. Unpresidented effort. But it will heal the body so that we can go forward. We choose whether to b in our highest center or rather eat bad ener & go down to our lowest centers. Human is a very desired vehicle but who puts God & Love b4 food? Who takes care to keep the human form? 99% is poi anyway. Also have to b Forgiving & Loving. We have to Understand & b Giving or it will come back on us just like a boomerang. Will come back as a bad magnet immediately. Anger will hold us back. Hate is the ener of the base of Spine, the red of hell, the fear. All virtues r necessary especially in this new 2012 ener. They put us in the higher centers cause they r Purity. About the toughest we must resist is food & fixing bad weakenings. Then we can b very Happy, overflowing w Joy. Do right to Spiral up.

Love is all that matters/the pos emotions. All the Scriptures & Saints agree on the path that leads to success...pos emotions. Dont even talk about neg emotions which awaken the neg off limit centers. Life is too short. They dont need to b increased. Mistakes r made. Forget them & forgive the other who messed up too. Otherwise we stay stuck in negativity which will hurt our Spine. Saints say to focus on the pos. Turn on the Light & darkness dissappears. I do my mantra & listen to God. Wat He tells me to do. Helps me pick out the right action. That will raise my ener. why would a shrink know more than the Saints who know God & can experience the powers of God? After all These r Miracle Gods.

A 30' tall Himalayan Yogi, Goldenbeard, was vigorously eating the bad electricity coming out of the oside wire even w His mouth to teach the disciple to throw out the soft s plastic that was weakening him creating magnets in the lower neg centers. Finally the disciple realized.

We like to keep unnecessary 'necessities'. Attachment can b broken not by listening to theory. Once is enuf. But by applying the principle/removing from sight to basement stairs at bottom landing or shed. That way it will hurt the least until Air is good & we can trash it. Metal or any weakening weakens less lower. Best to get rid of it as soon as possible so does not take other things to s. But attachment can then b broken by being further away from the weakening ener. It is science. Attachment exists strongest in the neg centers. Why conduct a bad frequency just cause everyone does?

The Pure will see God. Pure in Heart refers to being in our highest chakra we have or can open. Is how to b perfect. As close to God as possible. Not in the neg centers of vice. We need to forgo our desire to overcome & our percieved path to overcome for a higher desire to b in tune & w God. Let God direct our Life. Turn on the Light. Then the Heart can b Pure cause negativity wont b able to touch us. Will then have less to deal w cause we removed things in our control. & the biggest is metal. All s has to go to b in our top chakra. Get rid of all s. Do wo. We cant do it thru med. We have to control our environment. Keep it safe & Pure. If we 'eat' bad ener, r around bad ener like Goldenbeard eating the wire, it will work against us. If we r down in our meds or in activity we create an even greater s magnet in the coxxyx threatening hell. Wat matters is the length & intensity of the time we r Up or down. Black meditators/ magicians ignore the down magnet but the white 1st have the Virtue. Purity in place & then do the med. 1st Up, then med. There is no other way to succeed. The bodily house of God needs a good foundation. Building a house on sand(impurity) will bring failure.

Most things can b done away w in this age of need for less. Many in past gave all away. But the 2012 ener dictates we live w in this new requirement. We now have to b able to handle Spir ener. That means that in our life the neg ener is not a factor. We destroy the down vice ener by living as God says we should. The mind will thank us cause this s creates unhealthy neg Spinal magnets where neg emotions & vice exist. W a healthy Soul, brain, Spine & nerves; we will feel lighter. It frees us cause the electricity from the s objects, the exchange of ener is very low(neg) & affects us badly. It takes us down to a crawl compared to where we could b. 'I ate too much; I can hardly move.' Most things wen hit by central Sun/God's ener lowered by our Sun b4 it comes to Earth, most things test bad. This I found out soon after 2013. One has to test real well. Get Up real good & test real well.

Like Goldenbeard, we 'munch' on bad electricity trying to overcome wen all we have to do is delete the bad neg ener by Wise actions. B a Munchkin instead munching on God's Bliss & the other pos emotions. Throw out s. It is trash. Dont wish it on others or urself. Money can b gotten anew but our magnet cannot easily b reclaimed. Opposite actions will get us where we need to b. Fix the weakening like the Pros do. Like the Saints. Like taking a vacation, a retreat from life & enjoy the new scenery. Soon we dont want to go back to work. Back to attachment of or ignoring weakening things. There is a kinder way than ingesting bad things thru mouth, nose or body. We need to eat pos ener. Not become poi. Wen we med or pray we have essentially taken a vow not to hurt others & to live by the Natural law otherwise if we take in the bad, take in impurity; it takes us down which hurts us & other people, animals, plants. This is why the dark does it. They want to hurt others/devolve them. They dont consider the foundation so they melt cause they r practicing black. An attraction to objects over Love burns one up. We r wat we eat. Cant eat bad ener. God's laws dont change. They r the building blocks of the reality so They cant change. We hurt others & ourselves w our neg electro magnetic poi terribly even if noone feels it. So if we choose impurity, we side w having a bad magnet. We choose. But the choice is now. We now bet a Free. That is it. We make a conscious choice just to cut out impurity for the gift of Life. I'm Free. Cut out the iky frequencies & actions that cause them. Throw them off of us! For God present 24/7 in our Life in the greatest way. Is the high way & the highway to God. Such a good feeling is w us always. Cause there only pos emotions exist. This is not religion but the science of good & bad(ener). We have to make the effort to follow the Saints. Wat it means wen Someone died for our sins is that He showed us the way to b perfect. Showed us 'the Way, the Truth & the Life.' 'These that I do u can do & greater.' Now u can avoid the wrong way & succeed. B perfect. Even powers. Cant get safe by proxy. By another's effort. Wat happens to cheaters in school? Neg magnets have to b raised by living the Life. Is not a Free ride. We still have to work very hard to maybe make it. We dont overcome. We change our actions to get a better result, become perfect & r saved from hell. Why fall thinking ur thots will save u? Thots change. Feelings change instantly. It is the Spine that matters. Keep a pos upper Spine so u can handle God's pos Spir ener.

The worst weakening is a power station & 5g, then high tension power lines or s human. Lesser power lines. Then metal close or above us. The Heart has a brain. Ie is semi robotic. It can help us. Like a God fuse box in AI. We must listen to its Wisdom. These weakenings affect the Heart. So all ener matters(ie electricity of body or objects). It does not just dissappear. The Spine & brain conduct electricity. Pos helps the body & neg destroys it. This electricity in body interacts w oside electricity for a certain outcome which lately(since 2012) is neg. The oside electricity & our electronics pull our ener even more down creating even greater magnets in the lower centers that destroy.

In order to turn pos, one has to negate completely the neg effects which one cant do by proxy. One may feel great, xrcise wonderfully but the true message is in the Spine & fings. Learn how to get Up & then learn to test getting accurate results. In testing properly we will see the Truth of the matter. A scientist does not ignore the Truth. He runs valid tests that will reveal the Truth. If the thumb is weakened, poi is piling up quicker than being eliminated. Or it could b too much food or liquid for the body. Fix lil problems now, avoid sickness/big problems in future. Drugs in food like root vegies & rice & any others that have a toxic load affect us. These days never ever eat rice. One might as well b eating root vegies. Very many toxins have the opportunity to get into rice. Every Drug put into a comode. It is grown submerged. These r not normal times. We have a hard time finding non poi raw for enzymes even.. nanas. Or food lacking in fat, sugar, salt & poi. 99% is toxic. Why would we put it in our mouth? Wat if someone wanted to poi u, would u help him like Freddie did or would u fight for ur life? The body cant handle xtra trash. Poi & xtra water hurt the thumb, the elimination & the nerves. Is toxic for the nerves. & Heart. Anything that hurts the nerves hurts the Heart. So wen buying it is good to test the thumb. Poi will hurt the thumb. Some Drink lots of water yet die early. The body cant handle it. The body has to dictate the amount. A 5 min test would not hurt body as would Drinking xtra water. Wen water is too much, the Heart & kidneys, Spine & nerves r under unnecessary strain, the lower body can swell from xtra salt &/or potass cause of excess water & gravity. It pulls down the Spinal ener creating sickness & wears down the Heart for years b4 most can feel a neg effect. But this is shown in the fings immediately. One cant drink much water & have enuf milk. They dont sell organic milk powder usually. Commercial milk has 24d unless u can test real well & find where it got accidently bypassed. No wonder people & animals cant have poi s commercial milk! Is poi. In Heaven or Angelic realm Saints r lanky cause this is the healthy state for the body & the Soul. Excess causes magnets in the lower centers.

The reason we r weak or cant do this or that or control eating is cause the lower centers have too much ener. They should have none. Lower neg ener is the tool of the dark. This is where they can reach & hurt us. All wat they have is neg ener. The ener needs to b in the upper Spine where they cant touch us. For Saints, all in the 7th. The ener needs to b raised by Purifying, Fasting, doing right. Wen it is raised & in the upper centers, hunger, weakness & desire do not exist. Only the pos emotions, a wonderful feeling of fulfillment & higher sounds like the Rahn, Ra, Ram or Amen, Om, Amin. Or Horn, Trumpet or Ocean Roar(5th-7th); Bell, Gong(4th). Listen to God music. We should not listen to sounds below our stabalized chakra. But the dark poi everything. Or fatten, salt & sugar it to mess up the ener.

I have a way to rid toxins; the best way wen a person is in the lower centers wo hurting their magnet...cysts melted away, wen I gave them very lil water. Testing every bite & all liquid will keep blood pressure ok. Test for need. Suprisingly maybe on some people where there is an abundance of water, not much is needed wen there r bad magnets. Body knows. But we must correct our magnet so that we can get liquid to wash out the poi from the body. Body has a chance tho now to expel poi water that contains these cysts & things. Old water out, not quickly push out new untested water wo processing it very well cause the body cant handle so much. Wen we dont force body to overwork & expel newly drunk water, this is wat brings longer Life. Easy on Heart. Cant run wo the fuel pump. Fasting, giving body time to expel & rest. Calmness is achieved in body this way. Xtra liquid is hurtful cause it is the blood & liquid in legs which increases the s magnet increasing stress. Same w blood sugar. Good blood sugar brings calmness & healthy nerves. This is why putting up feet briefly helps to lift the Spinal magnet. LIFTs the liquid. Liquid conducts the s magnet at a time wen one needs to dry out the clothes of the Soul, the body. The Heart is hurt by excess liquid causing a more severe s magnet never having a vacation. & also xtra liquid is used to our disadvantage wen metal or other objects's ener hits us.

All objects have ener. This ener, either pos or neg, does not just dissapear. The neg creates weakenings that affect the body especially one that has xtra metal & liquid. Like pesticides put in fields, or chemicals in the Air that gets in ground water. Does not just dissappear. U cant just wash it all off. Even w soap. It is thruout & it has deformed the very thing it got into. The object is no more Pristine. Changed forever.. corrupt. R we Pristine? Is our ener pos? Or corrupt, deformed, neg? Spinal deformity whether scoliosis or other is NEG Spinal ener which causes a deficency of Ox.. Ox starved. Helps to create loose skin. Need pos Spinal ener for Ox to function right. So wen u have neg ener it is imp, it is absolutely necessary to supplement w Pure H_2O_2 or Dr Ox. Do we carry xtra water weight that hurts us? Do u know if ur shower water is safe? Does it contain aluminum, barium/carbon dioxide/rat poi? How bout raw jet fuel? Did u test? Is ur baby bathing in it? U? Wat is worse, the water or using a metal filter that transmits s frequencies? Can u rubberize it? Wat if the pipe goes 2 s? Cant leave it attached. In most cases the metal filter is worse. Can I reduce the amount of showers I take to not absorb so much poi? These weakenings need to b addressed. They can b tested & fixed. It is about fixing ALL errors propagated by the dark. Choke the dark who has u in his mouth about to swallow u. Choke by right. By perfection in all we do. This is how we make neg ener dissappear into pos ener in this life where we can do it.

Poi, too much fat, salted, or sugared hurts us. Pulls us down. It is vice/trouble. There is a cannabal who ate people's meat b4 the 2012 ener shift who lost his Soul & became a fallen one. But there is an ape I saw on tv who had his Heart chakra totally open who will b born a human next life. He was very Gentle & Loving & did not show animal characteristics like hunger, etc. This is how we should act to b Up & test.

Words have vibrations. Rahn is very pos. Cheerful has a real good vibration, Freddie, Bill, Sun, God, Carol, Tom, Mary r pos. U can test words on ur fings to see the effect, whether it takes u up or down but if u associate a name thinking of an s person w that name, it will take u down. Words that take ener down have a very neg ener vibration.. Wifi, 5G, name for a fallen one unfortunate enuf to have lost the fight. Red & yellow r lower colors. But if we r stabalized in the Heart, green strengthens us. For Throat, blue strengthens. Indigo for 6th stabalized people. & purpl for the Saints. Strengthens the Saints. The Spir Eye is Gold, Blue & White. The bad Spir Eye, wen we go toward the coxxyx is red in center & yellow around the red. It is repulsive to look at. For those who feel ener, the lower ener in stomach & belo is repulsive to feel.

We affect people around us in a neg way if we have magnets in the lower centers. We hurt them altho we have taken a vow not to hurt others (med or pray w a down magnet destroys since 2012 & we r trying to lift ener instead). Our neg ener hits their ener pulling them down. If we have an s magnet in our lowest chakra, we hurt others. This is the most hurting center. It is OUR freewill to rather choose actions that will undo the neg ener in our lowers. We need to get totally Up. It is not ok to practice black.. to hurt. We must build our bodily house on the bedrock of Purity instead of meditating making the coxxyx more neg, more toxic & hurtful, more destructive to our Soul, others & ourselves. The Gurus & Saints dont want that. 1st the DOs & DONTs, the POS emotions, a STRAIGHT Spine. Once we r in Heart or above cause of the 2012 Spir ener beamed, then we can med successfully cause Miss Purity is driving to the North pole of the Spine to b w Santa, our Saints.

Look at the grocery stores. How many r leaning over their cart w only their coxxyx left wearing red/cant stand up? Their nerves half destroyed. Shopping, buying indiscriminately, cart is full wen 99% is poi. How far forward is the top Spine or r the front hips thrust forward w Spine straight as a board w shoulders behind the back wearing royal purpl? Fact is the Spine has to b fixed to get from 4th to 6th again. Repaired & nerve diseases healed. Brain healed of brain fog. Dr Ox to the rescue. Instant concentration. Why? Cause u need Air to concerntrate. This is an attack from the dark to destroy. For the Soul we have to fight our way to UP.. Staying Up in the higher centers. A healthy pos Spine the Soul has to have.

Wat we die w that Spinal blueprint is wat our Soul is left w. We cannot b reborn in the next world or even later here wo regard to that blueprint. Animals same same. So why put them to death? Will mess up ur ener too. That could b a hell sentence. The blueprint governs where we go. How far does our ener go up? Is it out of the coxxyx & other neg centers which can take us to hell? We have to create pos ener in life. Dont think of s people or s Saints. Most r down s. Stay away to save urself. So let us have a straight Spine. Brace the Spine. If we bend, ener goes down, even ener in upper centers. It gets cut off.

7th people r locked into safety, They cant fall below human. They dont go to hell. They have worked out much of their karma. But if they fall to Heart, it is s for them & a forbidden place to b. We should not listen to 7th s people cause their voice weakens & will take us down to s. Also much music has a very bad vibration & will take many down if they have the lower s magnet. The singers many times r down s. So it is good to b aware of this & b very careful to notice if the singer stays Up thru out. Singing is dangerous cause u can attract an s magnet. If one is an expert on staying Up, they can easily tell if someone is Up or down. We can see the effect a voice has on our fings. We can listen to 7th people & Healers while They r Up. Sometimes it happens They get down, pulled down by the crowd. Then we can not listen to or watch Them anymore cause They would pull us down. U r wat u think about. U assume the magnet of who u think about so it is exremely imp to only think of UP people. That is the purpose of thinking only of God. God is always Up but One that comes to Earth is not always. U r known by the company u keep. & in this age of everybody being pulled down extremely bad by the oside air, it is even more imp to watch not only our company & neighbors but also objects. Ie air, food, objects in house, chemicals, everything.

2 Saints, a Devotee & a Dog

There were 2 Saints, a devotee & a dog who lived together. Saint Goldenbeard lived in the living room that He used for meditation & prayer w His Granite Starship, one lived in the kitchen that had only 3 walls. The devotee lived in the attic to escape weakenings & b all alone but had to go under the kitchen to go to the bathroom(purification). The dog wen he could went in the living room to b by the Granite Starship altar cause he subconsciously remembered being there in Atlantis w Goldenbeard, the living room Saint, as a man. But the now dog could not always go to the living room cause someone had chained his feet together. The metal weakened him terribly. One day Saint Goldenbeard decided to break the chains.

Having lived in Atlantis, He took all kinds of crystals, brass, forks, zappers & even a tiger eye bracelet to help the poor dog who had to breathe the oside Air at times, breathe the spraying of the sky. Goldenbeard even had Marble, like in the Taj Mahal. He took all the Brass He found that still had a pos vibration & hung it on the Granite Starship chimney wall to amplify the Granite. He sat the Marble on the mantle. He arranged all pieces till He had max pos ability throwing out wat had turned neg for max Spir ener. He had a platter of a rare copper that transmitted the Sun's pos Spir ener & arranged it too. He even was able to use the Titanium. Now he had a very powerful Spir antenna to pull Spir ener in from the Sun. He was able to change bad ener into good pos ener. He did it on a Watch & even on some food. Goldenbeard tested the crystals but the Sun had already over powered them. The crystals could not handle the greater & greater ramp ups in Spir ener from God. They radiated very neg s ener now; made the devotee's ankle hurt & go to sleep. So He pitched them in the trash container oside by the road. He found that even the forks & zapper had quit in their functionality & tested s so He put them in the shed out back so they would not reach the house. He then got out His most prized tiger eye braclet made by a friend for Him. But the Sun scaling higher & higher unfortunately took away its functionality also sending it to s. So to the shed the devotee took it. & then He called the dog to give him his Freedom. He asked the dog if he wanted Freedom. The dog said yes, he just wanted off these yellow chains, like bars that kept him in the porch kitchen (oside his Father's home in animal jail). He wanted to come in out of the trail bom bs & med in Peace & Happiness in his Heart. He did not want to b chained any more & would do anything to b Free. So Goldenbeard placed the dog on the Hearth & told him to say 'Im Free'. As soon as the dog said Im Free, the chains flew off from the huge Spir Brass antenna. Goldenbeard had pulled all the Spir ener in from the Sun to dissolve the lil dog's chains. So the dog medded(meditated/silent prayer) there on the Hearth w Saint Goldenbeard every night for the rest of his life.

The devotee not wanting to Purify in the basement under the kitchen decided to build all 4 a bathroom in the corner of the living room. By day the dog went upstairs were it was safe & slept w the devotee.

The kitchen Saint was moved by the dog's healing.. the chains had just flown off. The dog was completely in his Heart center. The Kitchen Saint decided to close up His kitchen so He would b only inside His house w God as it should b. The kitchen Saint saw the right way to live & realized that His friends were more imp to b w then oside His home by Himself. He threw out all that the Granite fried to s the day the dog got Free. So now everyone was warm in God & at least for now no one had to go anymore out. They lived together, helping each other putting Love 1st over wat they wanted. Goldenbeard turned the dog into a human & the devotee He saved from certain death. The kitchen Saint liked his inside home & had given up the oside life. Goldenbeard multiplied His living room w His Granite Starship & got the kitchen Saint out of the kitchen. They then had a very powerful group. The devotee, saved from certain death, started healing. The dog man lived Happily in the attic by day & medded in the living room Granite Starship w the others by night. He never forgot his healing cause he lost those terrible yello chains. He kept saying 'Im Free'. They had a simple life, trashed everything for a high living room Life in God w Goldenbeard. This helped their health, Joy & Bliss so much they decided never to replace any of wat got fried to s the day the dog got Free.

One day years later some people came by inflicted w metal bullets & icides from the giant's w a r. There were 10 of them but they also had metal weapons. They took everyone down but Saint Goldenbeard cause there were so many & also they were loaded w metal. The dog man screamed for help & the devotee nearly died so they both went up as high as they could go in the attic to get away from the s people & s metal.

A policeman came by & asked the devotee if he had called 911. No said the devotee. The devotee stood up & nearly passed out. So he got his Dr Ox & put it on himself & the dog until they normalized. Then the Pyramids took effect. Goldenbeard had gotten out His Brass again & decided to protect His friends. He had some Brass & Marble Pyramids & had the kitchen Saint reflect Spir Light up thru the Pyramids right to the devotee & dog man. The s people oside did not like the Spir ener & did not even realize it was there. They just felt more nervous from going down further. They automatically left to fight the giant's instigated money w a r & were never seen again.

Moral: We must b inside our home in God... in the chakra we developed +1. If we r on the porch or Purifying in the basement bathroom(neg ener centers), we dont have God's full Grace. If we decide to come into God's living room in the upper centers as high as possible, we can automatically heal & advance. God does most of the work. He can stand in us. Like He does Healers. Oside in the lower centers even wears on a Saint. Why purify oside or in the basement wen u can get much further in God's living Chamber. This is where the Bliss & youth is found.

In this new age of all the objects that weaken, metal & electronics weaken the worst cause it conducts like electricity. Antenna shaped metal will transmit more than solid. Ie. a metal shelf w a mesh of wires for the shelf. The shelves will then transmit all these bad frequencies in a greater way than a solid shelf. Electronics weaken cause of metal in them, bad waves they transmit(an s human voice can take u down if u r not Up good) & waves that go thru the Air. Cell fones r probably the most hurtful electronic over used for fone, computer & tracking. They hurt us cause they r a constant neg companion. Why would u need modern capabilities of tracking that hurt even the animals who r forced to wear devices? Or tags. Is better for a dog to keep his Soul then his master of this life. Testing will show u the effect of any metal, if it is grounded good, if u should keep it or throw it away. The more we limit metal &weakenings, the better off we will b. A devotee lost the ability to b on the internet. Her reward was none. No internet.

We can see if grounding metal into another object helps(lessens the weakening on our Spine). Ie, a metal chair weakens but it seemed to ground against a heavy metal legged kitchen table by touching 2 chair legs to the metal table leg. Eyes r weakened less testing both ways(testing fings sometimes & other times objects). A pan setting solid grounds or discharges the neg ener better if sitting firmly/evenly/solidly on stove.

Metal & electronics fry our brain. Look at all the metal in body(possibly even on centerline) & oside of body that is electrified by the neg & pos frequencies which escalates into a VERY VERY NEGATIVE ENERGY. & the metal furniture, metal cars, metal air- even if we dont breath it, it is close by. Like 2nd hand smoke. Still an effect. We r attacked by 2nd hand smoke & mirrors. Tricks. Metal conducts bad frequencies so best to b as far away as possible. Metal if not s conducts bad s frequencies & can easily go to s. If we have a big empty simple house, that is the ideal. Far from weakenings that we can easily fix. We need it on several acres so we can also have a green house far enuf away.

Even young people r beginning to realize these laws & the implied dangers. Some fones even have a METAL FRAME on top & weaken off the scale. Rfid warnings r being ignored even by the manufacturer. Since 2012 THINGS r differant, TOTALLY DIFFERANT. Test ALL & it will b revealed. But wen DOWN, can get WRONG RESULTS. Ie, tests GOOD wen really BAD. We r told not to touch water w live down electric wires yet arnt we doing that by carrying a load of toxic metal & liquid in our body? Down metal amplified by xtra liquid fries. Is a good time to cut hair & nails short. Bad hell frequencies abound in the air. They cause many new diseases, even autism. Our body conducts these. Being lanky like the Angels limits the bad effect. Wired metal shelves act as an antenna & bring in the bad frequencies. They r trash. Easy to get bad results w such a huge weakening. Test carefully.

We r here to LIFT the MAGNET. That is our sole purpose. & We r OUR BROTHER'S KEEPER here to help, not hurt them. Neg ener hurts others & ourselves. If we react to a person w a down magnet by eating, then we r escalating the problem. Food contains toxic metal that makes the problem worse.

The DARK r here KEEPING US from succeeding. Metal lamps r toxic anyway but also conduct electricity wen on. Unplug & ground hotel lamps laying them down on the floor if possible. Can block w non s wood. Huge metal dishwasher? Why? Wen one can wash a dish or 2 & tested plastic spoons, have one simple plug in light socket & b in a much more invincible position. We all have freewill but look at where it got the dark. They r failing. They wont get by w anything but unfortunately they will take many w them who want to claim they r weak. Only the strong survive. God's laws r the building blocks of Life so success can only b had by right. This is documented in the fairy tales.. The wicked witch melting into nothingness in a pool on the floor wen contacted by the Good Witch, the Spir ener of God. & then the pool dissappears. Bad witch became a fallen 1(ameba).

Weakenings usually cannot take one down but s metal & s Spir Brass(copper 87% & tin 13%) antennas can for many people. Even s crystals. Spir Brass can b used as a Spir antenna to contact Spir ener.. a powerful way to fix weakenings via testing. But if one has a lower magnet, the Brass will go to s cause of neg ener of the lower magnet person.

Wen man is at w ar, he studies the enemy to stay alive. He does not hang out w the enemy. Today life is full of impurities(enemy vibration) that separate us from Peace & Happiness, Cheerfulness, Love & Joy, & Bliss.. from God. They r severe infringements that prevent proper uptake of water & Air. There r 80000 toxins. U have icides, hormones, face cream poi, nana poi, fuel, 24d in most commercial, aluminum in Air, drugs of every kind...a very long list. Have a water problem where it just hangs around in the wrong places? Or brain cant think? Face raw jet fuel is dumped out of wings in the spraying of the sky. How do u get it totally out of well water? U cant but u can get it 80% Pure. There r toilet prescrip & other drugs, even nerve gas in food. Breathing rat poison is not good. Barium combines readily w CO_2 in Air & body. All these corrupt transient violations! 99% of soil is not fit to grow anything. 99% of food is not fit to eat. Why would u put it in ur mouth? But do we inhale the rat poi like Freddie or do we test our food for poi throwing out wat is not fit to eat? We cant take the money w us but we can afford to trash s trash. & filter the Air for God money u have 2 take at death.

S metal weakens less maybe inside drawers or in closets grounded(layed flat so max touches/a firm contact). The lower the better usually. Does it wreck the floor too bad tho? It can make other things go to s, especially wat it touches. Needs to b trashed as soon as possible. Keep trash can by street tho so less weakening for house. S metal may weaken floor & weaken u walking on it. Can u put it on a bottom landing till the Air gets good? Do the best u can to fix the weakening. At times lay down & put up feet to escape the weakening some. May weaken less on floor then up high in a cabinet(ideal place is at the bottom of a staircase till air gets good). We have to test to see. But a one story(no weakenings from bottom floor) w floor 6" above the Earth or slab(keep objects from going to s as easily) w brick siding(block out emf to a certain extent) is a healthier home. Wood floor can b built grounded/solid. No base or crawl space below u w objects to weaken/nothing above the base. Can ground metal on floor wo the whole floor going bad hopefully. Metal inside concrete still weakens/just less. Needs 1 ft concrete cover in all directions for metal reinforcements not to weaken. If concrete slab, wood floor needs to b 6" above slab. Slab would ground weakenings better but there would b more weakenings since slab is right on the earth. Brick siding blocks some of the bad frequencies in the Air oside but windows let them in. Do u really want windows in w a r time? 2 ft dirt walls do block out emf in the bottom 2/3 of wall.

S metal needs to b thrown out. The Pros throw it out b4 it takes the rest of Their stuff to s or wears on Their Spinal magnet. Is only money but our magnet is irreplaceable. Moving s metal or other s objects to bottom of basement stairs(wont weaken floor as much / separated by wall) or shed(better if far enuf away) is a good way to lessen the weakening. Metal & other weakenings weaken LESS there. B higher than the weakenings till u can trash it. Neg ener goes mostly down. Doors & floors block out only a bit tho. METAL affects EVERYONE very badly. Is very destructive. A weapon of mass destruction. Metal conducts.. a scientific fact. For 100% of the people. If a small wire can conduct such a great force as powerful electricity that can fry us, can u imagine how much Spir ener a big metal object can conduct negatively?

There r many unnecessary s things we HOLD ON to but we r being PUNISHED for KEEPING them. We r hurting our very Soul. The Galactics say it is a time to throw things out. If possible w all metal, another material would b a better option. Soft plastic needs to b limited also. Goes to s easily. A blanket that does not absorb face(non s wool defaced/cotton absorbs) would b better than soft plastic to set ur hands things on(touch only w bare hands). Or even defaced wood/a non s board. Metal cans, xtra bottles, metal lids, wire twistie ties, metal clothpins, paperclips(y not fold papers in 1/2?), staples.. most metal containing objects r not absolutely necessary (can find a better solution) but is necessary to keep the Soul. Clothes tho nice, many r s. Why not keep minimum for work & trash the s to not hurt others or ourselves? Objects can go to s anytime. S clothes will take ur good ones to s. & also wreck ur magnet. We must feel the ener change. Is it s now? Then toss.

We make a choice to hold on to s & stay down but this is not best health nutrition. 'Eating' s frequencies is as bad as eating s food. It does not matter how we get to s but that we r s & need to get Up. We can b Free this instant & THROW THOTS OUT which is the only thing that helps. Rid of ego all at once. Some thot is necessary but endless thinking will not solve anything & will take us away from God whereas if we do our mantra, think of God who is Up or an UP Saint & have only pos emotions, we get Up better & the solutions will come to us instantly from God. Unite w the pos frequencies. Their(the Saints) job is to help us. They serve others. Live our life as much as we do. They will think thru us or 'talk' us if we think of God & put God 1st. Do right. They can even shine us(send us Spir healing ener). The Saints do not interfere w our freewill. It is pertinent if we want to b all the way Up to concentrate & keep only the finest, the Pure gold of God, the pos ener in our highest chakra. If we toss the neg, we have FREEDOM from the LOWER Centers. We choose Love. We choose not to hurt our family w our desires or our problems. METAL & ELECTRICAL CLUTTER(ex. wires cant b all knotted up. lay flat on floor & separated) CAUSES ATTACHMENT cause it CREATES BAD KARMA INSTANTLY. Ie, neg magnets in our Spine just like sex, drugs, icides, chemicals, alcohol, many others. R addictive Drugs. Pure alcohol will leave the body but 24d(roundup in most commercial food), for example, will put s spots in ur sight until u undergo a streneous 10 or more day fast(will take some spots out). people also find themselves addicted to aluminum preferring Drinking from cans to glass bottles. U may think 'But Im not perfect. U shouldnt expect perfection out of me'. But in essence u r violating others & urself so u will have to pay. Attachment mostly exists in the neg centers where people r not allowed to b. B ye Perfect.. in the upper stabalized center plus 1.

But it takes wanting to get rid of metal & other weakenings. YUGE MISTAKE to hold on. One cannot stay in the coxxyx for more than 3-8 years wo having devastating results. Cannot b safe w God w a coxxyx magnet. God is not gotten by proxy like so many want to believe. They r led by the dark. Believe the dark. The example was perfection, miracles, fasting, right. Now let us do that. Raise the ener to human.

Major things can go wrong even just from objects weakening. We r known by the company we keep, even s objects. Why this weird attraction to objects? Trash s. Environment is stronger than will. We also have to let go of ameba thots. They r not ours. We have to pick the right way & fix the weakenings, not the convienient way. The Soul has the astral Spinal centers & the body is its clothes. We cant afford to go down. We wash the clothes in day by drinking 6 big glasses of liquid if it tests to get poi out of the body not overdoing liquid. 6 glasses liquid a day is usually enuf. 8 glasses may b too much unless u work & sweat immensely in a hot summer field. Testing will show the amount. Big business thrives on us overdoing liquid so they can 'fix' our Heart & kidneys. Only testing can accomplish this 100% safely. & at night(after 4pm) we must wring out the clothes to dry(fast on Air) constantly changing the clothes thru dancing w a straight Spine, putting in back & xrcise which raises the Spinal ener. Xrcise takes the ener out of the Spine into the muscles so wen it goes back, it goes where it should b - higher. Jumping unpacks a compressed Spine. Keep Spine straight. The problem w inversion or pullups is Spine can b thrown out of place the wrong way cause back is not braced. Jumping jacks weaken, r an unnatural movement. Never do we normally move both legs or both arms at the same time.

These days the problem is the spraying of the sky. Breathe & inhale the metal & u might as well b at a bar inhaling the fallen amebas in the drink. At any rate both take you to the base of the Spine. Wen the spraying started in the late 90s, people's ener went from being down in the Heart but still human or a bit down in the Throat, etc to being ALL in the coxxyx vice, the bottom Spine which is the center of hate & fear. Is the hell center. I saw this universal reaction to the spraying of the sky, a very evil looking ener. So this breathing in of metals is not conductive to testing. The results wont b as good but it is a start until you fix this leak in your pos Spine & bring the ener up thru following the laws of Purity & Virtue. Breathing toxic metals is not Purity. One needs Purity to see God. In other words, helping others instead of hurting even inadvertantly. It is still hurting others. Wen u have a calm, wen u do right, it is easier to b Happy cause the ener will naturally go up. The reason for right is to have Up ener. So we r Happy, Pure & the ener comes up helping others to b Up.

There r many things like the spraying of the sky taking the ener of all people down to the coxxyx cause they breathe or take in the impurity. This is not the will of God & the Saints, God's staff. & it should matter to us too. We must do God's will!

The spraying of the sky takes the Soul out of the bodily home in higher centers to s(coxxyx stone magnet). Have to avoid oside Air unless the Air tests good. Xrcise inside. Change central Air filter every month for any that snuck in w u. Dont use ac or oside Air to heat. Wen u go out cover completely. Cover every inch. The skin absorbs. Otherwise your fasts will itch & u wont get as far. Lungs(Dr mask that strains out the best) & eyes need special protection. How do u see when ur goggles fog up? Is a problem. Dont go out is the best solution. In most big cities they r 24/7 except for a couple hrs a week, sometimes a bit more. Wind takes the spraying of the sky to every part of the country & every farm & all soil. All the country is hit. Every part of the globe also from the nato spraying.

Test the open sky away from trees or electric lines, etc. They can b made invisible & wavy. Wind can blow them in. Rain can either clear the Air or bring them down. How the Air is on horizon is how it is for you where u r. Bad means they came down. Can test high up to see if a cloud or sky tests bad. Even the best area, South America which used to test good since they do not spray, the spraying off of aircraft carriers on the coast has reached the intermost parts of the continent now. All the world is affected, not just nato countries.

I go shopping wen the Air is good. This is wen we cut our lawn. I see if there r old trails from yesterday in the morning wen I 1st check. To test the Air, look at the sky in the direction u want to drive. Test open sky away from electric lines or trees.. I test a long time to see if it is good. I watch for the 1st spraying of the day to see how much time I will have & I come back b4 they come down. wen I see the 1st spraying of the day, I know they will b down in 5 or 6 hrs, maybe 7 or 7 1/2 if it is warm. Wen people complained about the lines in the sky, I noticed that they started to make them invisible. The Air tested real bad but no trails were visible yet there were those same trails. I could tell by their frequency.

During the budget dispute the summer of 2011 they could not spray the sky & all summer we were free to go oside until they reached a resolution. We had our Life back. But towards the end of summer the dispute was settled & the spraying started again. Later several times a hurricane stopped them from spraying.

They can make them straight, invisible or wavy. Wind can distort them 2. Wen they 1st make them, they come down to the ground after about 6 hours(5-7). After 6 hrs the clean Air is now toxic at ground level. After 12 hours after they spray the last, the Air will b good. So wen they quit making them one has to wait 12 hours to have clean Air. If one uses oside Air to heat, quit & use electric or a system totally inside instead. But one has to limit metal of all shapes & sizes severely to survive.

It takes 12 hrs for the room fine particles to fall to the floor. It's ok to come in quick. The furnace that does not use oside Air will clean that up(stay away from door for some time). An oreck Air filtering machine will also clean up the Air. We used one in the garage moving. Took 15 minutes but then the garage Air tested good. Look toward a blank wall to test the Air.

The spraying of the sky has a devastating effect on the Spine. Wen a person drops from 6th w 7th open to 4th, it feels very devastating losing their Spir sight. Like a tall person wo enuf clothes to cover their old Soul. It is the Soul that is all of a sudden bare. A life where there r no more Spir experiences like b4. No Bliss. Just animal instincts like eating where one may smell fire cause u r on fire... sulfur, nerves. Too big of a short. U smell matches. U run to find the fire but it is in u burning ur Spine & nerves up until the Heart nerve snaps & u die of a Heart attack or something. All caused by neg ener in the lowers, a recipe for hell. There one finds others in the same boat & is tortured by constant action & evil 'people' interfering. No rest or Peace. They look for some Peace in church. Church there has very lil Love cause they did not attract enuf in their actions on Earth. They lost their Love/Heart center. God has jailed them. They suffer cause of the other fallen. The fallen amebas being one celled r in drugs & chemicals. In all poi. Wen wc breathe in or consume these, we get possessed by many amebas. We possess the it who has a mind & desires of its own. 1000s can be in our body crippling our will.

So hell is a yuge mistake. So why not learn Patience, Purity & all Virtues so we can b Up? But we set ourself back so bad thinking we r incapable. Purity & all the Virtues have to b practiced as a human to insure the safety of a higher Life. We can get a bad magnet just by being next to someone w a bad magnet as in an apartment or hotel. In an apartment there is a bit more distance but increased metal. Anyone next door can dump their s dumptruck magnet on us. We dont even have to know they r there. Test the walls to see. That is why Paramahansa Yogananda said we live in human chicken coops. Too small. Some help can b gotten by blocking metal that u cant thro if in an apt or hotel w non s wood & sleeping 5 ft up. Also unplugging all & grounding(set solidly) metal as low as possible & being on the top floor. We need at least several acres & not so many things close to us. These days objects weaken. An s person's magnet or high tension power lines can go 1/3 mi or more. Power stations 2-3miles. Then there r emf pulses from haarp(controls weather / see website) in Alaska that go world wide. This is the enemy's world designed to wreck us. But huge bad magnets r created by overeating & violations of Purity & Virtue.

God did not intend for us to live in human chicken coops. He does not want chickens in coops either. The Soul needs more distance. Many houses r very close. Way too close. Bad magnets take us down. We need our neighbors to watch our house but at a safe distance. Everyone should b allowed 3 acres & the house should b in the middle on ALL

SIDES. Residences should not b built to maximize profit but maximize the Soul. Is a very deep need noone should b deprived of. In the isolated country it can b dangerous. But country Peace can exist in outer subburbs where electricity is underground & land is given to each house. Proper shelter is a very deep need. But we have poi food, poi clothes & poi shelter; many not even wanting better or knowing better.

House weakenings r from oside from others & inside from us. Both have to b fixed to survive. Then house wood if we r lucky enuf to have wood is poisoned 1st by the spraying of the sky & later on way to market. Insect poisonings r overdone wen tested boric acid alone will end termites, etc cheaply & wo poisoning us giving us a hate magnet or sending them to hell. Can b put where pets dont go. The lil ones cant escape poi like we can. I would rather have wood rot than me poisoned. Why is this poi w all materials? But who protests??? It does not have to b like this. I saw one commercial one time only about a man who did not want junk in his drinking water. It was quite funny & to the point. Was censored off tv. We need an awake population that demands perfection. Not 33% Pure water or even 80-90%. Stuff adds up. & u can go into a diabetes attack just from taking a hot shower. Other diseases too. why b a trash can for big business? Why give big business our health & ultimately our life & Soul? Topically use Pure water & get ur daily 6 glasses from nourishing food, not water, so u r kind to ur Heart.

Do we get a shower filter that will go to s fairly easily & weaken or do we take an occasional shower w unfiltered water? The filter may soon go to s. Wen s, is very hard to block w rubber in a small room up high besides it can take the pipe to s & then u have a huge whole house weakening. We have to weigh which is worse for shower, a weakening metal filter on shower, replacing it w non s always unhooking it after a shower or the toxic metal, fuel etc in the water. I opted for no filter drying well after shower immediately. If the shower filter goes to s, it can make ur whole house pipe go to s. Would really b impossible 2 rubberize. So much s metal in such a small place would weaken tremendously. & some would b up high. Metal objects r just too toxic & my water was worse than 80% Pure. But get a water quality report. On shower filters, Berkey black filters remove 99% of everything nearly(only 80% barium which creates rat poi). But floride, bacteria, virus r mostly gone. The Aquasana only removes about 45% floride. These r the only shower filters I know that even tackle floride. Do these remove aluminum, barium combined w co2(rat poi) & raw jet fuel? Not enuf but fairly good. But does the water have these things in it? Yes. Is the water tested for these?

They dont test for everything or even every yr. Nebraska has water that catches on fire yet the water quality report did not flag a problem. people haul big barrels of water to their home courtesy of big business. Cause of the terrible big business pollution. It gets very cold there. But testing can help u test city & well water. U cant take spraying of the sky out totally but u can dry 1st thing w paper towels or cloth towel washing out the face towel frequently. Do not let the water dry on u if severely poisoned. I opted for less metal((has a devastating effect on our bodies) & less showers(once a week) staying inside not getting spraying of the sky filth on me. It attracts amebas & tornados cause it is poi.

Courage is a virtue & the opposite of fear. Raises Spinal ener. Who will stand up wo using fear from the bottom fear center? We can act as if we r courageous. Shakespeare said 'Assume a virtue if u have it not'. Courage is in the uppers, God given to fight for survival. We r our brother's keeper but do we protect the lil ones who have no defense? Pesticides on plants? Poison food for animals? Or do we feed them vibrant food that helps them thrive. Why give them a possible hell sentence? We r not allowed to hurt others. Will hurt us. We must help them & we must hold on tight to God. I hear the animals complain wen their baby is shot. They mourn out of Love as if human. They r close. Very evolved. Horses fensed/jailed so they cant get rid of flies? They have no hands to push them away. why put them in such a small area? Abuse gives us a bad magnet & we might find ourselves lesser than the animals in the afterlife. Cause of God's beamed Spir ener, losing our Heart we will go to hell.

Wo being in our higher centers or at least somewat, we cannot get accurate testing results. The more Up we r, the better the results. So it is not wise especially now in this Spir ener to dabble in the dark emotions... hate, anger, stress, impatience, greed, fear, doubt, blame, judgement, etc. We choose our emotion. Transmute stress. Feel the pos emotion instead. Calm, control over our eating. We have to eat to feed the body. Greed(too much concentration on food) will eat us, will end our life putting us in hell. We dont overcome. We dont have to. We transcend. We just change our actions to the right action until they become normal/habit. Wat torture it must b to have lost ur Soul! They did not keep their ener in the Heart or above & r now still suffering the consequences. Truth has to b lived.

Very very many 6th or 6th w 7th open people cause of the spraying of the sky & other reasons, keeping the ener in s have fallen to the 4th & r in serious danger of hell. If they can feel their ener in the coxxyx, they will realize how food lowers ener like sex. Eating food is sex equated & they dont even want that. It is drugged. Is full of all kinds of drugs but any neg ener will drop to the coxxyx not just cause of 2012 & drugged food but the Spine is broken. Neg ener goes more & more down cause the s magnet has already been created so ener easily flows there. Only way to stop it is actions that reverse the ener taking it up, not down. This takes unpresidented effort. Pos ener. Pos extreme effort. We cannot b addicted or drunk on food. Might as well b smoking. & food causes a drug like addiction creating in the brain chemicals to b Happy. Fasting a week for control is the only cure. Or once a week or 3 days together each mo may b enuf. Meditation or silent prayer, not senses, is the better way to feel the Happiness, Bliss & Joy. God is in the stillness. 'B still & kno that I m God.' There r no side effects & it is Free. But w the s magnet in place, we have to med in activity. If not down real bad, do the Rahn 24/7 on out breath. Stabalize the ener 1st so it is ALL in the uppers. Months of pos successful work. Work then successful med. No bad consequences unless we go down further in our med or later as a result of meditating. That is practicing black magic... ignoring the lower neg magnets that destroy the Soul. Live Truth or pay. Need to 1st bring up & stabalize the ener in the upper centers. Once stabalized, then we can med but raise the ener 1st. Med w ener staying down is not good now cause of 2012 Spir ener & the overuse of poi now in our lives/Earth including corrupt emf, then metal & liquid cause of conductance. One should not feel or have any ener in the lowers. Down prevents u from feeling all the ener in coxxyx. If it is Up in med but goes down in activity, we need to concentrate on bringing the ener Up. Our 1st job is to have Up ener.

Now w 2012 & the ener shift the main thing we need is control over the ener. We r in a DIFFERENT WORLD SINCE 2012. Stabalize the ener, not bringing more Spir ener in. B in the higher centers so we can read & feel the ener. Down people cannot. Even if they feel the ener, they only feel a part of it & cant get an accurate reading of how pos or neg it is. Many down, even advanced people cannot tell if an object is radiating a bad vibration cause part of their ener is in the coxxyx (or their coxxyx Heart for 7th people) disabling their ability. But it is critical to know this so we dont poison ourselves w cures that hurt, not help. We may b convinced that it helps us but it does not mean it is helping us. We r just partially down & cant tell. I was surprised to find this out but it is now Truth to me that s people cant read ener properly even if they can feel it in their Spine. We have to test to see if it is indeed a pos ener & not trying to heal using a neg ener. But wen real sick, u can feel the good or bad ener effect of food in ur palm.

w 2012 & the beaming of Spir ener, things have changed drastically. We can sit in med but techniques r not needed to go deep & can b dangerous w the spraying of the sky & people's s magnets pulling us down. people around Paramahansa Yogananda did not med. They were in constant work contact w very high Spir ener(Paramahansa Yogananda's), much higher than they could get w a short med or even a long med.

Since 2012 we can evolve or devolve easily whether we like it or not. I EXPERIENCED the ENER RISING out of the Earth starting May 2012. That is why it is so IMP to b POS. Guru Paramahansa Yogananda would NOT let NEG EMOTIONAL people in HIS PRESENCE cause HIS ENER would HURT THEM. The focus now needs to b more on avoiding the spraying of the sky that devolves us or puts us in hell. It looks like a very evil ener if u can see the ener. It is a very clever tool of the dark. But God has some very clever tools also. I see the ener flows in people & animals. I studied pictures of dolphins & whales. I found out many were 7th. They r Saints to protect the oceans from evil. Nothing else could. That is why the dark had people hunt them & try to k i l l them all.

This is Drapara yuga, a new age of Aquarius, end of the Mayan calander(2012). In 1987 the Schumann Earth resonance was much different than 2012 or later. A 1st time physical ascension for Earth & fellow Earthlings. Ener came up out of the Earth starting May 2012. By Dec it was above the trash cans, trees & way up beyond. I saw this w my own eyes.

The pulsing of Spir ener from the Central Sun was then done. A ramp up & then decline in amount. This was to get us used to handling greater & greater amounts of pos Spir ener. Golf courses usually test real bad from the s(stone) chemicals. Wen the ener would ramp up, I would see the lawn go from bad to good & back to bad again as it ramped back down. Some rampings were severe lasting a day or 2. We would lay on our backs in bed to handle the ener ramp. Not only did we have that but we had the pulsing of emf from haarp in Alaska to affect our Heart(this has since gotten less) & also the weakenings from s objects that could not handle the Spir ener much less the ramps. Bodies r being updated from carbon to crystaline since 2012. Dna strands r being added. Instead of 2 we need 12 or 24 like we normally would have.

The Earth is going to the 5th dimension, back to Eden & God has decided to jail the bad(s magnets) & those that side w the bad on purpose or by default by doing nothing. By being weak. There r Galactic Saints Here to HELP in EVERY PHASE of life & also Ashtar of the Ashtar command in charge of a fleet encircling the Earth. Millions of vehicles as Paramahansa Yogananda said They would b helping us. They r mitigating wrongs, even some of the spraying of the sky to keep us alive a bit longer so we can fight to win the battle of Light for ourself. God is beaming ener from His Central Sun being stepped down by our 9th dimensional Sun to where we can maybe handle it. We need to live acording to law to make it otherwise we will b part of the disolution(Shiva the destroyer).

It is the state we have to attain beyond vice & impurity that is imp. That will give us God & 'These things that I do, u can do & greater'. Would not that b a great help to others? If we summarize all the Bibles of the world, it is about pos emotions, Purity, giving help. After all God is 1. Since God is 1, all religions speak the same basic Truths. Is our judgement & lack of understanding that sees differences.

Mother Mary in 1995 talked about this future wen she said for us all to Fast & pray. That many would b annilated. She was talking to all the Earthlings not just Catholics. She mentioned Fasting 1st cause all we do counts, whether good or bad. So let our eating 'prayer' b one of 80% full of TESTED NON POI food. Fasting is necessary to reap good prayerful results. Prayer wo Fasting has no meaning. Too much poi. Prayer wo works.

The Earth is getting Divine Ener beamed per God from the Central Sun of our Universe to our Sun & to here. It is critical to avoid the spraying of the sky, neg emotions & anything else that will give one a coxxyx s magnet. The Saints, AA, Galactics & other Worlders all agree on this. Saints can feel & see the ener in Their & other people's chakras. In order to b fruitful in life, one has to have fruitful meds &/ or a fruitful life. Ie, not in lower centers more & more but less & less till ur UP. Then one can advance. & only then. Paramahansa Yogananda said if u arent smiling to take ur fings & make a smile.. that it is that imp. He also said just b Happy. We must act as if. I teach to only have pos emotions. Avoid all neg ones. We cannot control our thots but we can control our feelings 100% if we choose to do so. This is the teachings of all Saints, all religions & all Bibles.

We have to practice Yama & Niyama... The Dos & Donts. Purity of body means absence of the spraying of the sky metal & jet fuel dumped from wings in our body which only creates neg magnets in our lower centers. Continence is not just w sex but w drugged food. Must avoid also drugs & anything equated to vice ener these days like emf. Icides & bad chemicals r addictive drugs. Aluminum & 24d r addictive Drugs. Internet & phone, tv, etc r addictive drugs. Everything equated these days to vice means metal, electronics, xtra liquid, emf, poi. Any mark of the beast coxxyx ener. Not easy but necessary 2 avoid vice equated poi energies whether poi or emf, metal or xtra liquid. Limit food severely.

In this present world it is very hard to b Pure. Wen we r Up & eat only what tests good; we will mostly b testing properly, intermittantly Fasting & all intake will have a pos ener so it will help(not hurt) us. Pos ener from eating only wat tests good leads to good karma or God cents, ie pos Spinal ener (the Soul's body at death) whereas eating out of want or food for food's sake activates the lower centers for a terrible afterlife. Digestion holds us down for quite a while. & we then join the terrible MASS karma of others. Have lower center magnets which have no meaning for someone on the Spir path. So many chemicals & poisons but this is wat God demands. Purity or go in the lower centers & have a good chance of a hellish afterlife. For the down 7th people locked in Heart & above, They can only hurt others, Their nerves & health. Purity is NECESSARY to b in the HIGHER CENTERS. It is a MATHEMATICAL LAW known by all the Saints. All Bibles talk about the need for Purity in the search for God, the source of all positive. We need a Pure mind & Healthy Spine. Need Pure Air. Need these to experience God b4 & after death. As b4 so after.

But people r not handling the Earth ener cause they let themselves b filled w metal & other toxins. Transmitting 4g, 5g, wifi...? One can only handle ener by Purity. Impurity pulls us in the lower centers whether it is food, a neighbor, vibrations in the Air, the poi Air, anger or sex. The dark uses many vice equated frequencies to their advantage.. wifi, 3g, 4g, 5g, other emf, electricity lacking proper ground & insulation, regular power lines, power stations that weaken for miles, haarp weakens worldwide. Also 2007 & later cars tracking, computers, etc. Even magnets, magnetic cards & bar codes weaken. High tension power lines should rather b buried no matter wat the cost(in Tx for 800 miles along freeway! Could not get away). Then computer, tv, radio, cd, fone, a long list of vice equated EVIL ener. Metal conducts tho & so we take on these bad frequencies on purpose(wen we do nothing) to ruin our magnet. Doing nothing is not an option if one wants to keep their pos human astral Soul ener body, the blueprint that the Soul has to have for a good afterlife.

So it is a channeling of the ener that is needed. So filter the Air to keep metal & fuel out of the precious body. Filter even store water. Is best not to drink purified or spring water (contains the elimination of bacteria & spraying of sky poi. Also the body cannot use inorganic minerals & will form s stones. 99% of all bottled water is toxic. Filter for Dr Ox the distilled. Face chemicals stick to everything so they can b a big culpret. Buy the best testing distilled that is filled to the top. Air at top lets bacteria grow & then u have their elimination(tests very bad). Home water may not b better. Testing is required. U would b surprised to know lab results on water. 1st Need or other very good filters can b used to filter distilled gallons from the store. After making a jar of H2O2(Dr Ox), squeeze out all remaining water from the filter b4 u detach 2 let it dry. Test the water after filtering to see wen u need to backwash. If u need to backwash, make several weeks Dr Ox so that the filter can dry totally. We have to have filtered distilled to mix w 35% fghp for our body otherwise we dont have H2O2. I do a glass at a time, put it in a clean non faced bottle protected from light adding the appropriate Dr Ox so germs dont grow.

Wen backwashing 1st need, backwash w not too bad city water from cold faucet. Pump water thru filter upside down. U can use 2 face free glasses. One for cold water the pump goes in. The other empty to catch the backwash. Refill glass again & again until u feel done. Can ask God & ur higher Self if u r done. Ur 1st thot many times is ur intuition peeking thru. Feel wat it says. Did 10 glasses do the job? Test the water coming out comparing it to water in the other glass. It is a little harder wo the metal accessories but I toss these so not to conduct bad frequencies. They go to s fairly quickly. Pump till no more will come out. Disconnect from pump, let dry totally. Pull up pump handle, turn different ways including upside down till ur sure pump is empty. Let both dry on good face free place. Rinse glasses b4 letting dry. The bad water glass could have sticky chemicals like face so wash especially good finishing w cold. The one used as input could have traces of face so 6 overflowing fills on hot & 1 cold would insure safety for both. Hopefully backwashing can get the bad filtered contents out. The 1st need has a very small hole that does not easily backwash wo the pump. Is expensive but a good filter used by top companies. Test how much better the water is after filtering.

W testing we can see if the sky is being sprayed. The toxic condition of the ocean or river can b seen. Testing will show u the hazards of soft plastic: baggies, gloves, etc. How bad do they weaken? Wen u buy non s paper towels or toilet paper soon the soft plastic will go to s. Wen ready to use it is good to put the paper on a table if possible on top of a sheet of plastic, defaced washed wool or wood. This will help them stay non s so u dont wreck ur magnet touching or wiping. W testing can see that s objects in a cubbord or closet will weaken less than out in the open. A weakening room will weaken us less in the next room w the door closed. Can see if the s object weakens thru the cubbord just by testing the cubbord door for weakening right where the object is. We can learn about limiting weakenings on body by grounding: an s baggy to b thrown away pressed down tightly in a cut off container or glass that is itself grounded good(set flat on table) will weaken less than if the baggie is just sitting there loose wo a good ground(pressed down). I use this to put weakening soft plastic in weighing it down until the Air is good. Then can trash the contents of the jar. W testing can see electricity thru the wires makes the object ener weakenings worse. & can see if the wires r grounded very well. Can protect ourselves by minimizing electricity at the breaker box or grounding wires better.

So in the beginning it will go slow but later one can test many bad bottles a sec each & AVOID ingesting POI. All NEEDS r MET in the testing cause the BODY KNOWS wat supplements we need at wat time & in wat amount. Sometimes 1/8 will b ok but 1/4 will b too much & weaken. We have to use common sense if our testing could b flawed. Wen down & havent tested pills like u should u could need 1 or 2. Nutrition, tho imp, is not the most imp. The imp thing is the effect of the nutrition on the body. That resulting ener is much more imp than any nutrition. A good example of pos ener overriding nutrition is the 9D spiritually pos Sun ener giving us D3, one of the most imp vitamins & from a Heavenly body. When there is only pos ener, our bodies function in a state of health & need very lil cause they utilize every bit. Neg ener makes the body go haywire not only w blood sugar but in all ways. It is the cause of Spinal problems. The cause of ALL problems, attachments & disease. In extreme cases, it eats up the Spine(pos ener), the Soul's home after death. Sciolosis & other Spinal problems r a result of neg ener.

Sweat, hair, nails, skin, elimination, everything weakens very medium bad to off the scale cause of all the toxins in environ. We have to flush about 7-9 times give or take for the weakening at the toilet to go away(2nd floor). Liquid flush a bit less. Have to test the floor by the toilet & see wen it gets a good vibration again. Otherwise it will wear on our magnet. A 1 story w floor 6" above the Earth(no crawl space) wont weaken as far but w a lower floor, can weaken quite a distance. After flushing, stay out of the bathroom several minutes to avoid the poi mist in the Air at the toilet absorbing into ur skin. Reach in to flush the multiple times avoiding the mist. The amount of flushing depends on the amount of ener in the ramp up or ramp down of Spir ener from the Central Sun of our Universe which is stepped down by our own Sun for us. These Heavenly bodies r named & worshipped correctly for God is there. Standing on s whether shoes or floor, our toe prints & arches r affected especially w a lower floor. On a wood floor 6 " above slab or Earth weakenings hopefully will not go very far.

Testing for s(stone) magnet is vital. Need to avoid s. Something is s if it tests worse closer to u than farther away. Even a little difference is enuf. Reason is bad magnets hurt us the closer they r to us. This is a good way to rule out store items that test fairly well. Poi is s. Wait 10 sec betw tests for eyes to lose intolerance.

But there r also clones. After Dolly I read a book that said a person was cloned so I found a picture of him & tested it. Clones dont have a Soul so they dont have Spinal ener. This person did all kinds of evil acts but still did not have a coxxyx magnet(base of Spine). I then looked at all the centers & found he did not have any ener in them either. All the Spine was totally vacant just like Dolly the sheep.

1 has to fix house weakenings wen they happen. At the store. stay to urself away from s people. The Pros get rid of s as it goes to s so not to give it a chance to take other objects to s or harm Their magnet. These points r crucial to being able to test.

The lifeforces in How You Can Talk w God(Paramahansa Yogananda):

1. Thumb-elimination, cancer, poisons, etc

2. 1st fing-circulatory, Heart

3. Middle-digestion, spoilage, virus, bacteria, mold

4. (dont wear rings)-respiratory/Air, Heart, lungs, virus

5. lil fing-metabolic, pancreas, thyroid, sweets, fats, blood sugar, bacteria

The 5 fings r linked to the 5 lower chakras. Thumb 2 coxxyx, 1st fing sacral, middle fing navel, 4th fing Heart, lil fing Throat chakra. The 3 biggest fings correspond to the

3 neg chakras & therefore will weaken if pointed toward head or Spine. The centerline in front is part of the Spine. Pos ener forced to vibrate neg shorts out.

If u put ur right palm in front of ur forehead wen down, neg ener will shoot out of the palm into ur forhead giving u a headache. It may take quite awhile to tell if one is not proficient. If we r Up in our higher centers, we can hold our palm in front of our forehead for as long as we want w no ill effect. The palm radiates the magnet we have at any particular time. Also wen down & hands r too close to the trunk there is a weakening effect from the neg hands. Move them further away & focus on pos emotions to get Up better, bend back, adjust back.

Since people would b receptive now using Paramahansa's lifeforce info(people understand more these days about ener. Is a new ascending age.), I developed a means of testing food, Air, anything as a means of not only advancement but to stay Healthy cause they r that closely related. Keep ur lifeforces in the fings strong (as Guru Paramahansa Yogananda mentions in How You Can Talk w God & in His Gita) & this can really help in having an Up magnet. So if we test to see what is compatible, we can advance & avoid all disease even alz which is just a lack of ener in the upper centers. A very serious disease cause it affects us in the afterlife. It affects our Soul severely. It separates us from our Soul.

To test, I created a scale of 0 to 21 where 21 is totally good. Trace(uu or oo oo -wat my reaction felt like) pesticides or weakenings r like 12 -20. Medium bad (uu shi)6-11. Shi or real bad if it is 2 - 5. Off the scale bad is 0-1. Testing is a way of evaluating the ener. We READ the ENER emanating out of the FINGERPRINTS or out of a milk jar, the Air or whatever we want to test.

Suppose u want to test honey in a glass jar, do not test at the label. Test the Pure glass where no honey is to see how it is & then test the actual honey by looking directly at it or putting your fingerprint directly on the glass where the honey is & testing the prints on the opposite hand.

Wen u cant keep looking at a fing u will know u r STARTING to SEE a bad effect. SEEING the FING vibrations CLEARLY can HELP u to AVOID & GET RID of some HEALTH PROBLEMS. Like if ur 2 Heart fings weaken or ur elimination weakens. Or pancreas. No sticking or money involved. This is free but one needs to spend time to get proficient as w anything. It saves time & Health by avoiding many bad actions.

Sugar including natural sweets like honey makes the pancreas overreact driving down blood sugar, whereas fat deadens the pancreas making the blood sugar rise. In the beginning wen the pancreas is strong, there is a tendancy to have low blood sugar. Later as the pancreas wears out, diabetes occurs cause fat has deadened the pancreas. Poi & electrolyte balance also affects the pancreas(affects all 5 fings). Wen there is a low blood sugar problem & for digestion it is best to eat the fat 1st to deaden the reaction to sugar & starch. Should always eat fat 1st cause of digestion. Then eating the other food. Fat & chemicals may cause the heels to crack if there is a high blood sugar problem. Cracking is caused by anything that sets off diabetes fairly strongly. Blood sugar problems take us down. Is the single most used method by the dark to separate us from God. There r many herbs & spices that level blood sugar. Can tell if u need more by seeing if the spice or herb will help the pancreas, the lil fing. Yogis dont eat onions & garlic cause they lessen calmness & usually r s. They also r root vegies poisoned severely.

Try to see how long it takes for the PRINT to WEAKEN ur EYES... u will want to blink or look away wen a bad ener is encountered. Eventually they burn. Wen the food is totally good u can look at it forever & u wont feel like u have to look away. It is a wonderfuil soothing feeling wen ener of eyes locks w good food ener.. how all food should be.

I am able to find commercial milk which tests good but many times it is off the scale bad. These days w a bad magnet or weakenings, it is best to buy week to week since neg magnets will take xtra food down. Orange juice or grapefruit juice & nonfat organic milk(organic safer if not very good at testing) is a fairly complete base. Nonfat milk, Seven Stars yogurt, juice(vit C), appl sauce, nanas, Yolks, chia. Those r the basics. A complete diet wen u test & stay in balance. Occasionally we need a part of a b12, d, b, bee pollen, del immune(acidolphus), coq10, msm, tumeric, a couple others. We would check everything. But our diet was pretty all encompassing w just those few foods. Milk has calcium & sodium. Juice has potassium & magnesium. These r the main electrolytes that have to stay in balance & will via testing so one doesnt get muscle cramps or go down. Fingers out of balance will hurt the lifeforces, stress them & take u down. Milk & juice supply the necessary liquid in 2 meals. Then at 4pm it is time to cut out liquid drying the body out. We had 6-7 hrs betw meals. Testing showed wen the food was digested & body was needing more.

I could have honey so I got a good supply of natural honey in the 1990s. Appl juice I sometimes found & I would get everything cheap w coupons. There was so much supply during sales that there was a better chance of it testing good. If a jar tests good, that is the equivalent of very many apples which one would have to test separately. & the fresh fruit seems to b dosed even more to make it look appealing. In 3 yrs the only fruit I found was one avocado. & I only found 2 chocolate bars, a couple tahani(sesame has protein). Mostly it was just those few foods that one does not overeat usually. God's foods adapted to the 2012 shift & the poisoning of the planet.

As w anything, learning to test is just a learning process but all we have to fight for our very existance. We will learn wat to do if we start applying the principles. ALL have the ability. Wen we only eat wat tests good we build a powerful force to protect us from darkness. Cravings fall off cause the temptation is gone & the gut has good bacteria so it asks the brain for more good food.

100% POS EMOTIONS r necessary to TEST. We all have the ability to control our emotions if we choose to do so. We have to b Up somewhat to get somewat accurate results. Tune in to ur BODY. How will this AFFECT it? Wat is weakening? Feel the ENER CHANGE around u. Staying Up is helpful in alzheimer's, ms & all diseases.

Testing 1 2 3 4 5 6 7 8 9 10

Testing steps

Prerequisites:

1. Positive emotions only.

2. Wear Dr mask for spraying of the sky so ener is raised as high as possible where abilities r. Metal on head or centerline weakens xtra/conducts destructive frequencies whether sky poi, jewelry, earphones... Same same for off of centerline. Still hardly much better: jean rivots(buy jeans wo rivots), zippers(cut them out), watch, tatoos, metal chairs... Trash metal & do not recycle. Soul more imp.

Steps:

1. Fix all weakenings, put Spine in place adjusting w the knuckles going up. Bend back till head seems down by waist(as far as possible)away from weakenings & s people b4 testing. To adjust neck, breathe in & hold jerking head side to side while hands r upturned, shoulder height fairly close to shoulders w elbows bent. Spine in will aid ur testing. Helps ener 2 go up.

2. test 5 min in beginning. Test long especially in the beginning, After u learn it can many times b just one sec to pick out a bad thing & 40 or so sec for good. Fast 1st then shop, Retest to improve accuracy wen u eat. Wen testing b an observer as if u r a Dr trying to care for a patient(urself). Observe impartially wo attachment. Dont go into emotion. Stay away from all s so it does not ruin ur magnet or ur things. So that u can gain in testing & b totally impartial. S is trash. Trash it to not trash urself.

96

3. Wen testing food, switch betw testing food w eyes & testing fingerprints. Will help ur eyes. W food look at it testing away from label. If all label, test white or least color so least poi ink. Wen using fingerprints test them while touching food w other hand away from label. Learn fings over sight so u can see the affect on ur lifeforces: Heart, pancreas & problem areas(spoilage digestion, etc). Test ea bite/swallow on Heart circulatory. Can't live wo the fuel pump. But double breathing helps digestion(2 in & 2 out w in greater than out breath).

4. Chew & swallow b4 testing next bite or swallow. Switch betw electrolytes keeping fings in balance: milk juice milk milk juice...

5. Dont touch food or test next bite while eating. Concentrate on chewing. Mix juice, appl & nana w saliva chewing many/ maybe 27 times. Then test next bite fully concentrating on that. Will it b milk or juice...

6. If tests bad or need other electrolytes eyes will burn or ull want 2 blink, look away or close them. Good u can look at forever.

7. If u need liquid it shows up in 4th fing, ur respiratory current. Too much liquid in pointing fing. These control blood pressure & Heart. All fings must have electrolyte balance. Eat fat 1st so digestion will b best possible. Undigested makes blood poisoning.

8. Dont hold 2 things while u test 1 of them.

9. Chemicals/toxins r s(vice/poi magnet) & test bad. Thumb picks up poi. U can rule out bad s food that way.

10. At end of meal check Heart circulatory & pancreas to make sure they r strong & electrolytes r in balance. This will prevent muscle cramps also besides a better UP magnet.

Points to remember

Do right; follow Purity & Virtue. Is the example of the Saints.

Evaluate if the lifeforces have a good or bad ener. & obey not eating wat makes ur ener bad. Renounce the food until u can have it. Body needs food from time to time. Let testing b ur guide. Eat wen it tests good so u can have God, success & Holy Health.

S tests worse the closer it is to u. wait 10 sec betw tests so that eyes will have lost the intolerance.

Sometimes wen I cant test, I test maybe 50-90 sec. Then I close my eyes a few sec & then open them to retest. Many times it will test bad very quickly. Am then in a naturally relaxed state & it flows. Must b Up to have accurate results.

U can test words or people on ur fings to see the affect of them on u. This can prove u should not think of s people. First see how ur fing is in the clear. U can tell if a person is Up or down by testing their chakras or seeing the affect on your lifeforces given in your fingerprints. Think or say their name and see. See how ur fings r b4 in the clear. B4 u think of them.

Strenthening or pos ener(God) u can also test on fings or by sight. Weakenings or neg ener of enemy test on ur fings or by sight so u can fix them. Trash s. The lifeforces in the fings affect ur magnet. If ur fings get bad ur magnet won't b as good. Is why we should test every bite keeping electrolytes in balance... so we thrive in Health having the best possible magnets we can have. Many have too much of both sets of main electrolytes. After fasting u will find the lifeforces r strengthened & r not so sensitive 2 electrolytes. I even can eat a whole meal calcium & sodium, then 2 more meals of the same. On 4th meal I have my potassium & magnesium.

Very little fat as in here heals u of blood sugar problems, etc if u avoid poi, emf & metal/xtra liquid. They cause havoc as if u were eating fat & sugar. A down magnet gives blood sugar problems.

Franken raises Spinal ener so more fat will test good but u have to test. Allow some of ur fat 2 b Franken. Franken & Lecithin/omega 3 r the best fats. Franken & Lecithin raise Spinal ener if they test.

Testing Scenarios

Not sure about olive oil. Test on thumb to see how many chemicals are in it. Test on pancreas to see if u can have the fat.

Need milk swallow but u r out & have to buy. U r buying juice but cant have it yet. Test for s(juice weakens more closer to u) b4 u buy the juice or go to a store that has organic nonfat milk buying that first & then after drinking max milk u can test juice in the clear wo the s test. But testing for s is a good way to rule out a food.

Dropped a dry mushroom on the car seat. It got faced. Do I put it in a bag to wash? Rather trash it cause face soaks into dry things. Poi cant b washed off. Is like face soaking into crackers wen they r made. Poi shows up on thumb. Shows up as bad for body.

Ur juice fell in the ice chest. Lid was on good but did water get into it? Test thumb for toxins. How is it on Heart circulatory? Middle fing for spoilage? Pancreas for toxins it does not like?

I need a Walmart 50 cents hospital roll. I faced my skin severely around the neck & wrists. So I bought a 50 cents paper towel roll. I put it in a brand new bag opening it slowly so as not to transmit face thru static electricity from oside to inside. Can face it all the way to the bottom of the new bag if u mess up. Putting my hands into 2 new face free baggies I tore off paper towels dabbing face off of me carefully throwing the towel down b4 it soaked thru the baggie. After half a roll in this manner I felt freer like I could do things. Is cause the lifeforces improved. Poi drugs the body taking Spinal ener down to coxxyx.

Respiratory current weakening yet liquid hurts. I needed electrolyte balance. My Saint who watches over me put a bubble around me shielding out poi & emf. So I have my Heart again & never get sick from the poi added to gasoline.

I ride my bicycle a lot now since I dont have to wear a spraying of sky Dr mask. The 3 ft bubble put me back into the good old days. After hrs of riding going to get milk my respiratory current was weak. I needed sodiun but had no NAC. Also the 1st store was out of milk so I opted for 2 coconut Larabars. They dont have 24d. They had enuf sodiuum to make my lifeforces good. I felt I would pass out b4 that. So I drove to the next store that had lowfat 1% buttermilk. I asked Him to take the salt & fat, s & poi out so I could thrive. He did. Why do they put salt in buttermilk? So my biking allowed me a couple egg yolks(Lecithin & omega 3), buttermilk(calcium, sodium & probiotics) & dried vit c fruit(He took out the sugar/was hard to find non sulfured but I did). I could only find some of the cranberries & cherries good enuf for him 2 fix. So this was my diet thanks to Him doctoring my food so I could thrive. I could not handle too much liquid. I had to pick the best I could find so He could get it good. & I always had to ask Him 2 so I could stay in tune w God will.

Vit c deficiency can cut the tongue. Test then & u will see c strengthening the elimination, digestion & respiratory lifeforces.

Im fasting & feel weak: Heart air(respiratory 4th fing) weakens if not enuf liquid. I could have several swallows of filtered distilled water that I had added some 35% Dr Ox 2 so it would not spoil. I tested from time to time for this.

———

Carbohydrates like beans & grains create a state where cancer & blood sugar problems can thrive including slime in the intestines, arthritis, joint problems & fatty liver. Xtra & poi settles in the joints & tissues. This may escape one until older or until doing a Dr Ox bulb enima. Not optimal whether grains, beans or else. Grains & beans r mostly s so they take the ener down. Soybeans cause of glutimate r conducive to cancer. Beans r sometimes hard to digest which means they r treated as poison by the body that rejects any nutrition they have. Grains r like sweets. The amount we eat of carbs would never test good. If we cant control the input, it is a food to b abolished. Cheese falls in this category. Too much fat & the stopping up. Accelerates cancer & disease. We r pretty much puppets following the Saints or the dark. Puppets of either Light or dark 'radio waves'. Is not our thots. So we should monitor our thots & discern where they r coming from, God or the enemy's fallen amebas. & ignore the bad ones. Then God can show u the way cause u used freewill to access good. Ask for help &

They can more readily help u. This is how u develop ur higher Self who u must learn to trust thru trial & error. The Saints want to help but They cant if u r not willing to do right, to pick Their thots. Saints monitor us to help us against the dark. Choosing right will save us many errors. A pillar of strength if we tune in. A true friend. If we hand our life to God, He/God can walk in our shoes even healing us. We r Free to choose best health nutrition or vice. Carbs promise Happiness but bring misery, fatty liver, cancer, low ener, slime & all kinds of disease. This is the way of the dark. But best health nutrition - all I eat is tested & compatible. I eat POS ENER. I am Free.

The reason Yogis eat mainly fruit & not vegies is cause of the s vibration. Vegies grown so close to the ground or in the ground naturally have the lowest form of life, the s minerals. The vines & plants dont strain out the s magnet as much as trees. This is why Yogis even b4 2012 eat fruit from trees, milk, honey & occasional rice. Much fruit today is s. Most avocados r s cause of the spraying of the sky. Chlorella can sometimes b found to take metal out of the body from sky, pans or watever source. So once diabetes is cured thru spices, herbs & fasting; fruit juice will b suitable for those people. They can drink the full glass of orange or grapefruit juice then. Hard to overdo juice unless u mix food. One food at a time like God made it is a recipe for success not being blown away by food for food sake. Pulpy C fruit juice is not much quicker absorbed than the whole fruit & can b found thru testing wen fruit cannot. It can b drunk slowly switching w milk & testing. Milk helps stabalize blood sugar.

Salt & sugar cause of their addictive qualities should not b in food. Salt has no nutrition & causes swelling which creates neg Spinal magnets. Excess liquid hurts Heart, Spine, Magnet, nerves, all. Sugar is much more addictive than cocaine. One food at a time. people w down magnets & a blood sugar problem should limit natural sweetners. Can decide betw blackstrap molasses or an iron pill for iron. No food is irreplacable. Wen we eat sugar & salt, we dont get our nutrition cause we r too busy eating the food that has added sugar or salt. But staples like orange juice & appl sauce(not raw w enzymes but can b digested easier since ground up) keep the body healthy. We should not minimize them. One food at a time brings success/God/progress. Desires, cravings fall off. We must make sure b4 we buy that sugar & salt r not in the ingredient list otherwise we lose control, quit testing & go down. & we take objects around us down & people. Maybe lose several pieces of clothes. This is not the way to succeed. We can never own much if we trash everything giving it an s magnet.. if we give things a trashworthy s magnet. We must b m-t(empty of desire as in the story of Goldenbeard talking the frogs). Even honey, even blackstrap molasses & the other best to b had sweetners that affect blood sugar may have to b cut out to b m-t. Stevia(forget the others that supposedly dont affect blood sugar), the best alternative(nothing added) still has to b non s & non poi.

The vines & plants dont strain out the s magnet as much as trees which many times dont either. Wheat besides being mostly s cuts holes in intestine & should b avoided. God made 1 thing at a time. Not all these recipes that take 1 to s. We must do as God, eat food simply to b w Him. Success is found in God's way, not hurtful food for taste. 'I m the blood of the lamb.' Sacrifice even innocent hunger for God. Eat meager we must cause of 2012 pos ener. Do things right. Live a very simple life. God pos ener can take s to safety..it takes much commitment to fight the evil trend. To bring God pos ener into the body. Live God truth. Not the easy way. Weak way. Weakness is not allowed. It shows up in the Spine. Sacrifice the innocent lamb(body animal) of hunger 2 b w God 24/7 right now. To advance. Japs & other Orientals quit eating at 80 or even 70% full. Much poi is also avoided that way. & 1 can continue human not hurting others w a down Spinal magnet. Takes Love not to hurt others. Love the Joy. Not value food over people.

Cows strain their milk to protect their babies. The milk & honey r filtered by the cow & bee to b as Pure as possible for the offspring. Goat milk tho considered cleaner unfortunately has milk fat thru out which never tested good. Takes one down cause makes people fat & helps create blood sugar problems. The fat cant b separated like cow's milk. One would consume too much fat. Body cant utilize fat & like cheese is stored as s until a good fast expells it. Butter is trash. If it was necessary for us, it would not clog the arteries but it gets stuck in the arteries creating havoc. 1% organic tested cow milk is most body can utilize. More will usually hurt the lil pancreas(lil fing). Nonfat w a yolk is better. But it must test good. Body can handle very little fat. More creates uncalm via blood sugar & nervousness from going down. Cow fat is not nutrition but hurtful to body's circulatory system +. Staying in body, it will go to s. These laws dont change from whim to whim. God's laws r immutable. The Fish Liver oil or Yolk was all we needed to digest the milk or yogurt. Those r extremely imp for Spine, brain & Heart. 'Lecithin in store got me Up better.' Tested Lecithin is Pure Love, opens the Heart. A spoon of xtra virgin olive oil is imp for Heart but not necessary every day.

Meat has the fear vibration of the dying animal. It stays in the tisses & goes to s. Egg whites too. Is lubrication from the birth canal-part of the chicken.

Oil is affected by heat & Air. Need to close cap immediately & put back in fridge so does not start going rancid. Slight rancid the body cant digest so one lands up w indigestion. Cooking w fat is not the best for Health(heat causes free radicals). All this shows up on the fings.. on the lifeforces thru testing. I could also find whole chia & flax oil that at times tested good. Omega 3 & Lecithin is good for the Heart, brain & the pos Spinal ener. Raises it. Yolks have both omega 3 & Lecithin.

Flax & chia have omega 3 & 6. Norwegian Cod Liver oil has omega 3 & Phosphatytlcholine as does Yolks. Phosphatytlcholine or Lecithin is very imp for Healthy cell membranes/anti cancer & pos Heart ener. Even 2 spoons oil(1 each meal) or one Yolk(maybe 2) a day is enuf w a bit chia. Norwegian Cod Liver oil has to b tested very well (but it is the most Pure). Yogis dont eat scavengers no matter how Pristene the waters r. They have s in the most Pristene places as in ALL ocean floors. These days s scavengers exist as most roots, most vegies, most nuts, herbs & spices r s. Test organic egg Yolks very well. Whether grain fed or pasture raised, 99% of everything is toxic. It pays to test closely. We can test thru the shell & the white looking straight to where the Yolk is. Each Yolk(12) has to b tested separately. They can b very toxic. Aluminum is cancer for the Soul. The DOWN Magnet is Spir CANCER. Bipolar is just a label for varying betw the s & the pos magnet. They get Up somewat from avoidance of the neg that pulled them down & r pos. Then from chemicals, etc; they go again down to depressed states. S magnet EATS UP the Soul BODY.

Hard boil the eggs 10 minutes to make sure they r safe to eat. One a day is enuf for most people. I ate 2. Hotplate timers r a big problem so have to boil longer to get 10 minutes boil in. Phosphatytlchlorine makes up half of cell walls. It also raises Spinal ener which helps sleep. If this phosphatytlchlorine is missing, the deficency will let cancer develop. Phosphatytl serine makes up 10% so it is imp to get these. In fish oil, egg Yolks. Phosphatytl serine brings down cortisol so you can sleep.

Nanas help sleep also. They quit weakening middle fing about the time they get spots. Green fruit of any kind weakens digestion & causes blood poi instead of nutrition for the body. Keep nanas from getting real ripe if u have lower magnets cause of blood sugar. Wen part of a nana bruises or rots, most if not all of the nana needs to b trashed. The bad has spread to good looking parts. Testing the fings will show this. Wen I eat the nana, many times Ill have to thro the bottom half cause of an imperfection that extends far into the good looking part. Can land up w some in ur mouth ull have 2 spit out.. They throw around the unripe nanas stocking but the damage is permanent. Many times the 1ˢᵗ & last bit r slightly bad too. Cant even see the bruise but yet it tests for 1. I throw that out cause I need totally good. But 1/2 a nana is enuf nutrition wen u dont use salt. Is even enuf enzymes.

Fat needs to b eaten 1ˢᵗ wen we have maximun digestion power & also to deaden the pancreas a bit so it does not overreact to the juice. If Yolk does not test good, try a swallo of juice 1ˢᵗ. Then test the Yolk. U may need to balance w milk b4 the Yolk. It depends on ur previous meal & other factors. Wen testing milk, test the actual milk. If all is label, test white(least toxic ink). Wen food has a bad vibration like w chemicals u will want to blink, look away or ur eyes will burn. The same looking at ur fings while testing the bottle, the better way. U can diagnose wat is happening in ur body. In the beginning it takes 5 minutes but wen proficient, one can tell in under a min if it is good. If bad, I can tell in just a sec. U can test w the left hand (receiving hand) or the right (ener flows outward). I test w either. Put a print on the food away from labels or on the white of a label if all is label. On the other hand see the ener of the hand prints. How does the milk affect my elimination? My Heart? Is it too much liquid? Is it spoiled? How does my pancreas like it?

LOOK at the CENTER of ur fingerprints. The PALM side of ur HAND. U can do this wen u have some xtra time like wen standing in line, etc. Most people's THUMB is bad from CHEMICALS. Cause of Health problems & medication the 1ˢᵗ & the 2 lil fings could b bad also(Heart & pancreas).

U can see if ur food is spoiled(middle). It is amazing how fast oil spoils in heat & Air hurting ur magnet. Leave oil out long enuf & u wont want to even smell the rancid. U will toss it. Oil needs to b frozen long term & refrigerated wen u start using a bottle. But why feed ur fings spoiled food that hurts every organ in the body cause u r more s w poi blood also? Test each bite to stay in balance HELPING ur MAGNET. Keeping lifeforces strong will make it much easier to stay Up. The body has to b held in balance to b max Up. Ie if u take a swallow of tested non gmo pulpy orange juice, the next swallow should probably b organic tested nonfat milk. U may need two of them for one of juice. We dont eat salt so milk will b more than juice. About double. The calcium & sodium in milk complements the magnesium & potassium of the grapefruit or orange juice. Sodium has to balance potassium & calcium has to balance magnesium. This is a pretty complete diet, these 2 things. Pulp gives collagen. Lack of control can escalate worsening of the fings & make ur magnet worse which will cause u more hunger than had u seen if u could have 2 juice in a row. But u may need 2 milk for one of juice to stay in balance. Nana has even more potassium. Follow the testing & you will see. Sodium & calcium must b in balance w potassium & magnesium in order for the fings to b best they can. Then the body can b max Up. & u will learn to feel if u r in balance. Add a bit of tested appl sauce, an organic egg Yolk in the beginning(fat 1st), spoon of soaked organic chia. This is a fairly complete meal w a nana for enzymes to digest. Occasionally test a d3 or B12, bee pollen, del immune(good bacteria) & a few more to see if u can take a partial pill. Or how much tumeric u really need or any food. No guessing. This is the final say on how food will affect ur health. It is scientific. Icides show up. Superfoods.. testing shows wat the Truth really is. Is it super for u? Is it Pure? Any food, was it wrapped in s aluminum or other s material or did it go to s cause of poi or for any other reason?

If something goes to s b4 u eat it, throw it out. It is the best & cheapest health ins. That & fasting. We can b YOUNG & HEALED from ALL DISEASE. Moderation, avoided chemicals by tested nutrition will bring a healthy youth. Inorganic salts & minerals cannot b utilized by the body as well as organic plant based. Some can b stuck in body unused & from the environment go to s. But why soak in the enemy vibration? It is a philosophy of ener, the only way to advance. Pos ener in & keep s ener out. Soak the body only in pos ener like tested Dr Ox or Franken & Pure food. Absorb Purity thru skin or mouth. These r not normal times. Is a new calander. A new cycle that never happened b4.

Milk has sodium & calcium. Orange juice has potassium & magnesium. Both make a nearly complete diet. So you want to check milk on the 2 Heart fings, the pointing & 4th fing. See how the lil fing is on milk(pancreas/blood sugar). Same w jui. So you optimize/try to get the fings to 21. Milk supplies much needed protein & organic calcium, & jui the C. The middle fing will show u if you ate something spoiled. Virus, mold & bacteria show up on the 3 lil fings. The thumb will tell u if u have too much bad to eliminate, have Cancer, too much inorganic, toxins. It is imp to get in balance so that the Spinal magnet, Heart & blood sugar r the best possible. Organic is safer. Has only the spraying of the sky which is toxic so food has to b limited. Animal protein is full of hormones & like the wind, they dont stay put so even organic milk has to b tested very well. We usually never drank distilled water(no stones) w all this nourishing liquid. Where else can u get such good nutrition? Certainly not tea which usually is s anyway. Has no c or protein which we cant live wo. Has no organic calcium or sodium which we have to have. Only a swallow or 2 of water a day would test good if that. It never tested good on me cause of all the liquid I drank. Wen thirsty or hungry, it could b a wrong signal. Like bad bacteria or a dark overlay. But body knows the max liquid it should have. It shows in the testing & it needs to dry out at night totally. No liquid after 4pm. Holding liquid in bladder while sleeping takes one down. Pure distilled water will not make kidney stones or overwork the kidneys. & kidneys underfunction anyway cause of all the chemicals they find absolutely necessary to excrete. Like salt, inorganic minerals may become a burden to the kidneys if overdone(there r natural remedies). So nutrients stay in the body. It is impossible for distilled to leach minerals from the body. It is a misconception. Poi will make u feel weak too. The body would 1st eliminate poison, not good biological minerals. I have seen many fasts & I know this for certain. I see wat happens in the body. Most distilled & other gallon WATER is TOXIC at the grocery store & in HOME filtration. So distilled for Dr Ox needs to b filtered for safety. Fruit made by God for us has distilled only. No inorganic trash. Salt is inorganic trash, has no purpose & causes by water weight gain a worse magnet. A great tool of the dark to destroy. Also anything that stays in body has a higher chance of going to s by staying in the body longer. Body is full of poi from all the chemicals, etc. The body takes what it needs & then some. God gave it that ability. Non organic minerals cannot b used by the body. They r trash & cause stones & s. They hold the ener down just like meat & egg whites cause they lodge in the tissue worthless. Inorganic calcium same same. Like vegies, most herbs & teas r s or have a great tendancy to go to s. They r too close to Earth's s minerals in the ground. These r not ordinary times. We have to work hard to succeed.

Wen I test something that is totally good it is the most incredible thing. I resonate w the ener. I shake my head Up & Down saying ya ya ya...a very Strengthing movement. My eyes lock w the wonderful ener of the object. I connect w the Pure, good ener of the food. Shaking the head no has a very weakening effect. Better to move fing sideways.

We need to Love the body by testing wat we give it. Not abusing but being a kind king ego. Just like we have to b kind & loving to others to b Up, for our tendancies we have to b also. So they help, not hurt the organs.

100% POS EMOTIONS is KEY to learning how to TEST. Enjoying & being Happy w wat we do gets us Up as good as possible for testing. The more Up we r, the better accuracy we have. & the better God can do our work thru us. We need to get Up as good as possible b4 we test. Putting in our back, bending back & other xrcises Paramahansa Yogananda & I created can get us Up as good as possible also. Both pos emo & xrcise/Spine in place r necessary.

It is a process of tuning in to ur body & how a substance will affect it. FEEL the ENER CHANGE. Could possibly find it helpful to put a left fingerprint on the food away from label & testing the right hand. See the resulting ener coming out of the hand toward the eyes. Does the food help or hurt that lifeforce? Is the best insurance you can have. Test each bite to stay in balance. Keeping lifeforces strong will make it much easier to stay Up. Results from not trying to test could b devastating.

God has ordained(2012) the Earth go back to Eden(5th dimension) & we also so we have to adjust to the fact that we have to control ener. We r affected by rampings of ener. Testing is a way of staying w in the pos ener. We READ the ENER emanating out of the fingerprints or out of a milk jar, or the Air. Left is receiving hand & right is sending hand. Right sends out ener. This is known & used by the Saints. But wen testing, u can use either hand or even feet. But best w down magnets to keep hands far away from trunk & head wen possible to not increase the down magnet especially the right which sends ener.

If we r real sick, we can put an appl in our palm & feel/tell if it agrees w us or not. To test u can look at an object & if you want to blink, look away or if ur eyes burn, it probably has icides or something that is not good like an s magnet. Could b u r needing the opposite electrolytes. Ie If u need juice w potassium & magnesium, milk w sodium & calcium wont test good so keep this in mind. But icides burn. Just open a bag of 24d & see how u do. We cant rely on feeling to test unless we have a very high state. Many times the 1st thing we think about something is correct but not always is it correct. We can fool ourselves.

The 5 currents show up on the prints. Put a print on a food away from the label. If egg Yolk, put print on shell. Or look at the food but not the label. If it is all covered(hiding something?), pick a place that is white(least poi cause no ink). Bend back so u will be up better & get more acccurate results. If food tests bad, could b u r down too far to eat. Cant digest it.

Do double breathing to ready the body. Also bending back will help to get u Up so that u can digest better. Bend back arms shoulder height out to side palms up till head feels down by waist. Gets u up better so u can have food.

If testing toilet paper(same for towels or qtips) for s, look at the paper or qtip, not the plastic it is in. look thru the plastic concentrating on the paper/qtip & u will pick up the ener of the paper or qtip. Also test the plastic where there is no paper or qtips to see how it is. If the plastic is bad & paper/qtips good that is a very good sign if the testing was accurate. If plastic good & paper bad then forget it.

A BETTER way to TEST at the store is to look at ur Thumb print wen Touching the Other Hand Print to the Food. That way u see wat is toxic for ur elimination & also if the food is full of chemicals. Can do for the other 4 lifeforces using the other fings. It will b easier to PICK UP ur SPECIFIC problems this way. U can do it. Everyone has the ability. Takes trying. Gets better w PRACTICE. I try to have MAX distance betw Myself & the shoppers so I can TEST BETTER. If someone is DOWN REAL BAD, they can take u DOWN some & wo u knowing it. Then u can get WRONG RESULTS.

Wen 1st learning how to test it will take 5 minutes but after u learn it can many times b just one sec to pick out a bad thing & 40 or so sec for good. If u put ur print on it, look at ur other hand & see the effect on your elimination(thumb) or ur Heart(2 & 4) or pancreas(5). How is the ener coming out of the thumb? Does it make u want to blink or look away? Does it burn, is toxic for ur eyes? Or does it feel ok the whole time? Is someone close who is s(leans over cart w coxxyx far back or wears red)? Or u can look at the food & see how it makes the eyes feel. Does it make u want to blink or look away? Is it toxic burning ur eyes? Or is it good?

In testing is the means to stop food poisoning(all 5 weaken). Virus, mold, spoilage, bacteria...the 3 lil fings. No guessing anymore. Just the science of ener. Oil spoils very quickly to Air & warm(immediately cap it & put in fridge). Once spoiled, it is not fit to eat & is trash for the system. Frying is not good for this reason & it also causes free radicals. Spoiled food cant b fixed by boiling. It will test the same & who wants to eat the trash of the bacteria? They test like trash. Rotten fruit also even if only part is rotten looking, most is rotten to the tester & needs to b trashed. Some people can have the SLIGHTLY spoiled food wen they have a lack of good bacteria but it will also test good for them. Food should not b left out but refrigerated. Food spoils quicker than we think. So we need to b Up to test. & if not Up, to get Up best we can by putting in our back including bending back. & not rely totally on the testing using common sense.

It is not possible wen u go down to get Up right away. U have to make the effort to b Up in the pos emotions which over time pulls the ener out of the lower chakras so u can b fully Up. If there is a Spinal problem also, bending back will help to let the ener flow up. Concentrate on Happy emotions & doing right. Brings ener up. If ener is Up we will automatically b Joyful. If ener is down, we will have various states of ill as in depression & sickness.

Moderation is the key. Can b Up easier if moderate. But many bigger people have a better magnet than slim. Virtue is very imp. Following dos & donts is most imp. Purity is extremely imp. why jump off a cliff just cause someone else did? If someone else messes up the Air, why breathe it? Cant b in a good place after death wo Purity. Poi & poi emf including metal & liquid conductance of them(they r everywhere) r vice equated. Ie mark of the beast. The black magician is shown many times w horns cause of the coxxyx beast ener. They r lost in vice, neg emotions & vice equated 2nd hand smoke & mirrors. In tricks to separate Soul even wo vice enjoyment for the k ill-Soul abortion(24d & aluminum, other poi r drugs). They r coxxyx ener, a very heavy ener. But food is vice & is easily overdone. Is drugged. 99% is poi. If food is a problem, the Saints have not condemned u. Wat 2 do? 'Go home & sin no more. Eat for body, not the mouth. Restraint brings the Up. Do the mouth ameba xrcises from Dr Ropes story of the Story book. Eat meager portions to supply body. More will make lifeforces in fings go to 0 wrecking the Up magnet. Do not overeat(will make u go down), eat poi, poi emf or metal/xtra liquid. Drop the weight for Immortality. Fast at least 24 hrs once a week. If the human upper Spinal ener is kept too long in bottom Spine, human abilities short out like a car battery touching human pos upper Spinal ener making it vibrate in the lower neg centers where heavy vice only exists, not Love. The human form is a much desired vehicle for the Soul & ego but who takes care to keep it? This drop in ener to the base I saw universally happen to people wen the spraying of the sky started. Everyone! No matter how good they were. So we must build God common cents in Spine...raise Spinal ener creating good karma. This is the meaning of karma, of advancement...where we r in Spine. & we do take this God money w us at death. We must b wo lower neg magnets pulling us down. The Spine is the exactor of the afterlife. This blueprint that we built in life we take w us. Is why some go to hell (if their Spine implodes/upper Spine shorts out & bcomes vacant/only coxxyx vice center left for a hell sentence/mur der of the Soul/in coxxyx too long not to short out). We can do all sorts of pos things that r termed good to do but if they dont raise the Spinal ener, that should signal to us to concentrate on just the most imp. Wat raises Spinal ener. That must come 1st, last & always b4 anything else. B Up fast forwarding 2 God in stabalized center + 1. That is perfection: stabalized center+1.

So we can test the sky away from trees to see if good. We get an hr or 2 of good Air a week, sometimes 5. W testing we can get an accurate pic of wat is going on. So learning to b Up is extremely imp. It is the best insurance for ur Health & proper testing results. A prerequisite for testing & getting correct results. 2 very important ways to b Up more r 1) earloop mask or better for screening out the fine spraying of the sky & 2) pos emotions. These 2 r essentials by all means to raise ener/accuracy. But many test down somewat & get much help. It takes time to learn to b Up but there r simple steps. Think back to that Happy lil girl or boy u were. To stay Up:

1. I am a Happy(or Joy, Bliss) lil boy(girl).

2. See everything as a test to take away ur Happiness(Joy/Bliss).

3. Ask God or Saints/ask higher self EVERYTHING that u do b4 u do ANYTHING so God/higher self's Wisdom can stop u if is not right & b Happy to do only right. Can get a Light overlay. Saints can talk u thru ur thinking.

4. If go down do #1 & dont do anything else. Dont b interested in anything else.

The currents show up in the fing & toe prints. The state of the Spinal ener shows up in the palm & arch as either pos or neg. The left hand is the receiving hand & the right sends ener. That is why u see pictures of people standing w legs apart & arms out to side shoulder height w left palm up to receive from God & right palm down to expel bad ener into the ground(best w down magnets to keep them away from trunk & head wen possible). Is a pose or mudra that helps to get one Up. It is the same principal as in the Pyramids where base ener is grounded into the ground in the square base & the triangles meet at the tip which is where the Spir ener goes up thru to arch eventually down to charge Ma Earth w pos Spir ener on the lay lines. Is a device used all over the world & even in my home to protect against bad frequencies.

Testing gives us the ability to know which milk or anything has bpa or any toxic substance. Ener testing is a means of reading this ener, avoiding the neg & creating compatible pos ener. Testing helps us b in balance w electrolytes(sodium & potass/ calcium & magnesium) for the best possible magnet & alkaline/acid so our life is smoother.. no muscle cramps or acidic environment.

Wen testing down u can get wrong results.. good wen really bad. We have to test very well to pick up icides & other poi. If an s magnet walks by while we r testing, we can get wrong results too. So it is good to check & recheck. Sometimes an s person is in store behind an aisle close to you, u buy but later at home it tests bad. Sometimes I test my shirt which I know is good on a place where there is no sweat to know if I can still test. Or I test something that I know is s & see if it still tests s like most store vegies.

Unfortunately most vegetables have the s magnet especially root vegies. plus they have added drugs from dirty water watering. Most beans & grains r s. Occasionally we did find chlorella. Chlorella can get toxic Air metals, molybdenum from scratched stainless steel pots or any other metals out.

If u keep your lifeforces strong by testing every bite, staying in balance w electrolytes, this will enhance ur Spinal magnet. The Spinal magnet will enhance the fings & this will create a euphoria. U will b Happy, Cheerful, full of Love & Joy & later Bliss. Why? Cause the upper chakras r involved & they can only feel these emotions.

The coxxyx is the seat of hate, anger & fear. Sacral is sex. Greed/food is the navel, the animal center. Animals dont like to Fast. Animals have 3 chakras active which can b seen by Saints. So in order to have a pos magnet & pos fings, we must have these emotions automatically or act as if. In this Up state it is possible to test food accurately to see the effect it has on our body. Is this food good for my Spinal ener or is it full of icides or metal & hurts the Spinal ener? Did something inadvertantly get into the organic? Does it have too much of the oside Air metals, fuel, aluminum...? Did they tell the Truth on the packaging? Is it wrapped in recycled(is s poi) &/or s material which caused it to go to s? Food is only as good as the cover/wrapper. Food is known by the company it keeps, by the wrapper so recycling is not good cause of all the chemicals. Poison is trash.. should b trashed. Same w aluminum touching liquid. Might as well trash that food. Almond butter stuck to the top aluminum seal? Trash it. Recycling is bad. Wind & people touching spreads poi, hormones, everything everywhere. Food was made for us. Not we for the food. Poi food should not eat us. Some even recycle used paper towels full of face cream & other chemicals that take a person to s. Not a smart move. & how would u eat any fruit that has face all over it? Nanas u can peel but that is it. The others u have to rinse in VERY hot water 5-6 times & then wash w soap not setting it down on face. How can u do that w a big watermelon? That is most likely s anyway. But if u dont, the knife brings face from peel to the inside. Even if u throw all juice u will still get some face. Knees can develop problems w too much poi. Knee operations can b prevented by avoiding s & poi if one is getting collagen in pulp of orange jui or supplements.

Testing can b used for food, the Air, Spine, even to see if there is asbestos in the house. Testing works cause we r dealing w how ener interacts w ener. Science says all is ener & this is true. Pos ener brings health & wellbeing. Neg ener prevalent today brings sickness & devolvement. Sickness & a terrible death.

How 2 fix weakenings:

Is possible in this toxic world to be bound 2 Up in 100% Purity. Avoid vice & vice equated energies. Trash all metal for ur Soul. Keep Soul rather. Rubberize wat u absolutely have 2 keep. Cant rubberize keys very well tho. Create Purity by testing every bite & fixing every weakening. This is post 2012. Is a new requirement to either swim in God or perish after death. Like Noah's or Sodom's time. A toxic flood. There r no Happy ghosts. They lost/were fooled.

Soft plastic & metal can easily go to s. Monitor things such as these testing ur things for a pos vibration. Try to feel the energy change. If ur fings r weakened, it could mean there is a weakening. Something went 2 s.

A weakening is wen there is neg energy especially coxxyx vice equated ener that takes u down 1st in the fings & then the Spinal magnet. The s wears on ur magnet. people can cause a weakening. Metal can really cause havoc cause of the enemy emf in the Air. Conducts. The s ener is trash. Sometimes a real bad obect that weakens will take other objects down. wen all objects in question r put far oside grounded some may recover in time wen u take the worst one away. is better to only have 1 floor, not an upstairs over a lower room. Ducts in basement weaken the whole floor above severely since they r metal. Objects need to b grounded or set flat. Like a spoon laid flat on a surface instead of loose in a tray. Things need to b away from the edge of the counter so they dont weaken the floor. Hanging over weakens.

All objects have an energy & cause of 2012 pos ener beamed, most objects radiate negatively. Or the Spine, cause of the spraying of the sky is forced to vibrate w coxxyx vice ener. Is not of God nor does God allow it. It burns up the upper human Spine. & nerves. If Heart center goes is bye bye to the human form. Soul abortion. Soul needs upper Spinal blueprint to b connected 2 the human form. We hurt others wen down. Is like stabbing someone in the back but u r just in their vicinity. Also if people think of u & u r down, u hurt them. We r supposed to help others, not hurt. Love them. We r our brother's keeper.

Some things that weaken:

24d, aluminum, toxins...

Many synthetic fabrics, most labels & elastic.

Metal on clothes, etc. jeans?

Most vegetables, herbs, grains, beans. Anything can acquire a neg ener. Testing is key to see wat went down. Is why in this unpresidented time to not think of others nor eat from the ground. Roots are usually very bad. Even trees many times cant strain out the poi. R s. Nuts & avocados r a good example. & out of season forget! Can find good organic sunflower or almond butter tho if a Saint gets it up. Some very occasionally is ok. Sesame has protein, can thro/dab w face free paper towel the oil & it fills u if u can find good testing sesame. But any commercial field food probably has 24d at the very least. Once used, it stays around. gmo & non gmo. Is not easy to get rid of. U can see that wen Fasting. So any commercial food has potential ka ki ller 24d & probably much more. It cant b rinsed off nor Fasted very well out of body. Eyes may have spots in sight for the rest of ur life that take u down. So commercial fields will grow food that burns up the upper human Spine needed for God experience. Is no Purity in icides that act like drugs. R drugs. Is impurity. pollution. These stay in the fields & our bodies for many yrs. 1st stop eating it. A very long Fast may improve ur spots in sight but not take them away. Or it may not get any of it out. I have seen both happen but mostly it staying in body no matter how much u Fast or sweat.

24d causes death in life. Dont u think it causes death in afterlife? Is a severe weakening many times worse than alcohol. But most alcohol now has 24d. Things r different than in Paramahansaji's time(has Final liberation). In Heaven there r many Gods who r

1 w the 1 God to help fight evil. Creator Gods turn desert to lush. Failure 2 success. Can create a mountain & take it away. Can 'talk' anyone thru their thots & control instances of their life.

Eating & meditation these days wen down has a terible affect on the Spine. 1 first has 2 b bound to Up. 1 goes further & further down practicing black. Toward hell. Cause of pos God ener being beamed since 2012 & all the enemy freqs of big biz whether poison or emf. R vice/satanic freq. Is why it causes disease. Metal & liquid conduct these destructive freqs. Meditation is very dangerous wen we cant even handle the energy being beamed. Practicing black is not allowed by God. There is nothing wrong w meditation. Is only silent 1 pointed prayer. 1 pointed concentration on God. But we must adapt to the environment that is destroying us. Do techniques that help, not hurt us like Rahn. We dont need more pos God ener. Saint ener is beamed to us. We have 2 learn to handle it. b4 2012 u could get up in meditation but now there r too many bad frequencies. Most people ignore their down thinking down ener is ok. But they create more & more of a hell hole to b another very woke up unhappy ghost who cant go into the Light. & their Spine in later life & many times early on show their deformity. Coxxyx further back. God does not allow deformed abused Spines. & Heaven is for those who become Immortal. Why have neg ener in Heaven? 'Be ye Perfect' is the commandment. U hurt people by the stone or s enemy magnet very badly taking others down to coxxyx vice destructive freq. s Spines caused by the destructive coxxyx hell freq at the base of Spine causes Spine to implode after a few yrs. Lose Spinal Heart between shoulder blades & u r no longer human. Is thru shorting out touching pos God ener to neg hell energy shorts u out like a car battery. man is a special creation as long as he takes care 2 keep it. As long as he fights to keep his Spinal Heart(Pure in Heart will see God here on Earth). Gives him the ability to put Love b4 food. Wen u raise the ener out of the neg centers, u will hear the sounds of the Gods(The 1 God has many Creator Gods under Him). Music of the spheres. Horn & Trumpet of Bible, etc. Bell is Heart & Horn 5th. Trumpet is 6th. Ocean roar is 7th. U dont want to concentrate on the lower sounds cause of 2012. Feeling Power & reverie comes w the symphony. The down r deceived 2 believe they have wen they dont. Must give up ego all at once otherwise amebas crippl more & more will. Cripple the will, b a failure still. We must wake up & do things properly. Right is the only way. Paramahansa unified Christ's & Krishna's teaching. Christ means Krishna in the Hindu religion. Christ & Krishna means the Final Liberation state in different languages/religions. This is when u have power to bestow the miracles. All ener is above the head gained by restraint. This is how u get to the Bliss of God. So they r the same if u leave dogma out. Is illumination. Can access God the Father from the Son aspect.

Intensity of effort is required for success. Up magnet is created by length & intensity of the Up. Once u develop it, will b much easier to stay Up. A down magnet by the same reasoning is hard to undo cause of the length u have been in it & by the intensity of ur down actions that hold u in the destructive coxxyx. Other people also play a role in holding u down. Dont think of others. Most r s. A mur derer can end ur life. Similarily ur life is affected by mur derous impurities that God wants u to use ur freewill to avoid.

Spir ener or God ener comes from restraint. It is easy 2 b impure. Restraint brings Purity, a very light ener. Indulgence brings a heavy neg ener. Look how the cow indulges all day never thinking of God, eating grass, digesting it in all 4 stomachs. These days food is drugged. Even w prescription drugs. Is poi. Why put it in ur mouth? Wen the mouth bcomes active, we lose Spir magnetism. But magnetism grows wen we keep mouth shut. Mouth takes ener into neg centers. Digestion at the very least. Fasting & partial Fasting helps to raise the ener. Wen the mouth bcomes active the eyes lose Spir magnetism. The face bcomes distorted & in many cases the body. Let the mouth rest & Spir magnetism builds up again. An animal does not think of God but food. Do we act as an animal? Is the test of Life. There Spir magnetism is nonexistant. Spir magnetism creates the Up energy. That is the purpose of testing every bite & fixing every weakening. So mouth never bcomes too active. Wen the mouth bcomes active thru talking or eating, ener is drained. Eyes lose magnetism that was gained in silence. God is found in silence. Close off the senses for the 6th sense, intuition. Here God is. 'I m the blood of the lamb'. Sacrifice the innocent animal tendency of hunger. Sacrifice taste. See God.

Amebas have no Spir magnetism but a repulsive 1. A terrible smile & a terrible END. R all in coxxyx hate/fear center. Beware of those that promote fear. R not all amebas. We inherit ameba lack wen we dont do right. Weakness is not allowed. Only the strong survive. It is ameba radio waves we tune into wen we do wrong. They influence us. Wen we think of someone we to a certain extent inherit their magnet, good or bad. Think long enuf & they can pull us totally 2 coxxyx. Or as far up as we can access at that time(stabalized center+1). So we should not think of other people cause they could b down. Up Saints have so much magnetism, They have ener shooting out of Their eyes. Is why wen people see Them they say They r so beautiful, so immaculate. Is more than skinny which They all r cause is required 2 b Up. They r very magnetic cause r perfect as we should be.

Testing every bite & fixing every weakening in home will get u well. Wen hands strong & magnet Up u wont b in disease centers of Spine & can thrive in Holy Health. Out of the 3 lower, will enter the God states, the wonderful pos emotions.

To adjust Spine keeping it Healthy as is taught in the traditional paths use a sharp stick pressing the vertebrea back in place lossening the calicification 'concrete'. Undoes fusion which is of the enemy, vice & impurity. Press back in. Make it crack. At the same time tense neck. Spine & head are connected. even ribs can b adjusted to help the skeleton/Spine/brain. Skeleton is required to b Healthy. This heals the head & Spine. There r other ways too. They r interconnected. Can see wat will crack or wat is the wrong way 2 push. If ener goes down or fings get worse is the wrong way unless there is another problem like a weakening in the room. Something going to s. Feel the ener change. Monitor the things in the room & trash them if they go to s. Take them oside at a distance. See which will recover & r s just cause the worst thing took it down. Cannot b down. Cause of the spraying of the sky & God's 2012 pos ener, will go all the way to hell burning out every center of Spine if human heart breaks. R just too many s fallen amebas, people & things/objects.

Wen testing for s, wait 10 sec betw the closer & further away test. It is s if it tests worse closer to u.

Soft plastic in a closed box, if bad enuf can weaken ur whole house. Generally tho, it can b put in a closed box, compressed down & stored in house. But not an unfinished basement where metal in the ceiling will b weakened meaning ur whole house floor could b affected. A box will weaken worse than the same thing in a cubbord usually.

If possible, use the old light bulbs that dont have a lot of metal rather than the metal ones that fry ur brain. They multiply the satanic frequency.

How do I know if a metal closet bar weakens? Test the oside closet door where the bar is. Will weaken if bar is s. Or a bedroom weakens? Test the bedroom wall from the adjoining room. There could b multiple weakenings. Test tne adjoining walls to locate the weakenings. 'Wrecked my med for the last time. Out u go. Where r u?' Put the s at bottom landing of basement stairs or on kitchen table or somewhere to ground so floor does not weaken(basement below). Test & see if where u put it if it weakens the house, garage door or house door or wall. For instance if bedroom wall or door weakens from oside the room, there is a bad weakening in line w the place on wall that is the worst. So b careful that where u ground an s object that u dont create another weakening. U dont want to weaken the garage, basement, a metal object or anything. May have to take far away oside b4 the Air gets good if very bad & cant ground. A Dr mask wear for the spraying of sky & cover every inch to keep the poi filth off of u. Testing will show u wat 2 do. Sometimes the s has been so bad, it went over a block(trash sac). Metal can go much further.

We cant forget to talk to the other person, God. It is just like living w another person. Can save us time cutting out useless actions. God can even help us fix weakenings. If we r in tune w God's principles the Saints can 'talk us', can talk very powerfully thru our thinking. Save us time doing right which brings success. We should talk to our guiding Saint instead of reacting w eating xtra food. Food takes the ener down(how far depends on anount of s & food). 'I fixed all weakenings but now my Saint cant help me get Up better cause ener is digesting food.' We lost contact cause of food for food sake.

Separate soft plastic from metal. Plastic & metal is a toxic relationship. They have only the hate/fear center. Separate by wood, paper, cardboard or the like. They r from vegetation which is 2 centered. Bottles dont like to touch each other. Nor do baggies like to touch water. They have not developed Love. Will weaken worse touching. This I witnessed by the testing in 2012.

'Some basement bottles r weakening my magnet. These clothes r s. This fountain is now s & is weakening. Mother Mary on marble goes. Is s. Moved s Dresser away from window so not to weaken metal eve. Have to resolve the weakening as I find the s like the Pros. Feel the changes of ener from good to bad. S Spir cross has no meaning.. is s. Keepsakes, antiques.. not worth hurting the Soul w them. Trash can can b full every week. Get rid of the metal eve. Has lost its value.'

Test an object & see how it tests. Then hold it closer. If it weakens quicker, it is s. Bad magnets hurt us the closer they r to us. This is why the Saints in ufos wen contacting Earth people keep a distance. Cause it would hurt the bad magnet Earth people to b exposed to the high Saintly Spir ener & also hurt the Saints who cant handle the neg ener cause it is very destructive. They r sensitive to the neg ener whether from people or high tension power lines. The higher the pos ener, the worse neg ener is for 1. The greys r alien but r glorified insects. They dont have their emotions developed. R not pos. But the tech is from the Saints.

If we have only one reaction (Happiness, Cheerful, Love, Joy, Bliss) to everything that happens to us no matter wat happens, we can stay Up, keep our ener in the higher centers & progress physically(Health, etc), mentally & Spiritually as long as we follow the laws of Purity & Virtue. Neg emotions hurt all systems in the body. Staying Up is the fertile ground for miracles to manifest. God performs miracles thru His Saints but only if the one receiving the healing is in the higher centers.

We have to b constantly Happy & full of Joy no matter wat. It takes a constant effort or vigil to stay Up including a straight Spine. This is necessary to stay Up & also to b in Harmony w people so they can stay Up. If we fear, r unhappy, impatient, or any neg emotion; we go into the lower centers of the Spine. We can always respond w Joy but we must b Happy, not just say it. Paramahansa says Happy like we just got a million dollars. We may not b able to control our thots but we can control our emotions. Everyone has the ability. We have to b willing. Thots can get us in trouble too if there is an underlying emotion or if the person u r thinking about has a bad magnet, ie. all ener is in coxxyx. This is why we think(pray to) God cause He pulls our ener up. If wrong thots come in, we must not have that second thot. Focus on Bliss, Happiness or Joy rather. So we have to:

1. B & act Happy (or Love the Joy, or feel Bliss). Love alone will not work cause it is too associated w sex.

2. See everything as a test to take away our Happiness.

3. Think b4 acting making sure we act Happy, calm & nonattached(m-t of desire) while doing God's choice for us. Then the Saints can work thru us. This is why Paramahansa Yogananda says to remove likes & dislikes. Do wat is right. Ask God everything b4 u do anything so God can stop u if wrong.

4. If we go down, #1 & b silent concentrating rather on cutting our losses & not going down again. don't b interested in anything else. Our magnet depends on

the length of time we r Up or down & the degree of Up or down, the intensity. Eating & then going down will lengthen the time down considerably. The lifeforces can't handle digestion wen down cause they r in a weakened state. Going down wrecks the fings. They r off the scale bad.

Relaxation helps to keep ener in higher centers. Tensing especially the lower muscles(hips) has a downward effect on ener. Best to b "calmly active, actively calm" as Paramahansa Yogananda says. Live life relaxed. If rush, b sure u r calm or don't rush.

To see the EFFECT on BODY, put print on METAL & then look at the other hand PRINTS to see the EFFECT on the DIFFERENT lifeforces. Like a fone or any metal. Metal goes quickly to s cause of the strain, the toxic load of bad frequencies since metal conducts. Metal & all things weaken less if they r grounded. Loose silverware in a Drawer each not square on the wood will weaken terribly. But a spoon touching the wood in both places will weaken less. If the object is too bad like a 10 out of 21, it many times is too bad to keep. These r things to limit to the least possible. If not s, they still conduct s frequencies. U can LESSEN weakenings by GROUNDING. Also LOWER weakenings r BETTER than HIGHER up. Neg ener goes down as in a Pyramid. It is the science of ener & the building blocks of this creation.. Metal conducts & if it conducts bad, it has a bad effect & most is bad now. Fries ur brain. So these effects show up on all 5 fings. Emf & even normal electricity weaken. We need to test unbiased. Is this good or bad for my elimination? Can I have more water or will my Heart weaken (pointing fing)? Something is either good or bad. Not just for one but for all people usually. Ie aluminum is bad for all even if they dont notice the bad effect yet. It is not dust people r allergic to. It is the chemicals in the dust that r not good for anyone. Pollen same same. Allergies for some means the thing has something wrong w it... the toxic additions.

Magnetic bracelets used to heal but now w mother Earth radiating Spir ener they weaken & I tested this. My light machine frequencies totally changed. I had to find where the good ones had gone to. This change in frequencies was universal cause of the Spir ener being beamed. Also things were no longer constant cause of the change in ener constantly. Ramp ups of ener. Then backing off. My good magnetic bracelets changed to a bad frequency. Everything changed frequencies cause of the Cosmic ener being beamed. The GOOD ener unfortunately Magnifies the BAD &

the BAD is BAD to START w. people have to starve to b right these days. Eat like a bird. Once habit, will b easier. At times u will even feel u got enuf. But test. Have to fight against the flow of evil. Of weak suggestions. It is a time of DISSOLUTION wen MANY WILL PERISH it was predicted. Mary said it so we would FIGHT, FAST, & PRAY. She mentioned fasting 1st. Is LIKE in Sodom & Gomorrah(Saints). God said find 10 GOOD MEN & NONE were FOUND. God dissolution. Saint Sodom's wife looked back at vice or even necessary food in her eyes & fell to hell. It does not matter wat takes us to hell. Wat matters is to abolish neg magnets to b safe in God. All neg emotions. Even greed for food will take us there. The spraying of the sky will take us there.

The Spinal ener body we have at death follows us to the AFTERLIFE. It is our ASTRAL BLUEPRINT, our Soul's body DICTATING WAT we BUILT in LIFE WILL FOLLOW US in DEATH to the NEXT. Or to hell. Ener does not just die. U CANT make an Angel out of a down magnet. There r many stories of lost ghosts who still cant accept hell & hold on to their last life staying in the home they died in. & if a SAINT has magnets IN LIFE in the Heart, Throat & Spir Eye; THESE FOLLOW THEM into the next. Ener has an effect. Listen to s Saints & u will inherit Their bad magnet. Even tho They r HIGHER THAN U. It is the type of ener.. neg ener. '____ was up above head HEALING MANY but later the crowd of people took Him down to s Heart & I could NOT LISTEN to Him. He WEAKENED my FINGS.' IE elimination, the 2 Heart(circulation & respiratory), metabolic & digestive which would take me a bit DOWN so I would not listen to Him anymore.

Wen people r influenced by others for the worst, it is a horrible mass karma. KARMA is the STATE of the Spine, the Soul's BODY. Who we THINK of or ASSOCIATE w, we BECOME. CAUSE ENER NORMALIZES. W 2 people, if one is WAY UP & the other WAY DOWN, the ENER WILL FIND AN EQUILIBRIUM. IF the UP person IS STRONGER & the s NOT SO BAD, the UP person COULD PULL the s person UP. BUT IF s IS REAL BAD, the UP person WILL MAKE the s person GET EVEN WORSE CAUSE HE CANT HANDLE the POS ENER. It is like a person throwing rocks at a Saint. His stone hits the Saint who is above head & like a bommerrang it flows back to the s person heavier & pulls him more down. Same principle as the weakening objects. S cannot handle Spir ener. The bad witch melted into a pool of nothingness wen in contact w the Spir ener of the Good Witch.

Many 7th DO NOT REALIZE the SCIENCE & have people concentrating on LOWER centers. They mean well. But wen u Concentrate on LOWER Centers u get a LOWER magnet. Or Saints concentrate on their Heart wen They should b above the head. It is SCIENCE. So WAT we r TRYING TO DO WILL NOT GET DONE CAUSE OF SCIENCE. HAVE TO PROGRESS BY GOING UP, NOT DOWN. NOT RELATING TO BODY. Ie TOUCHING BODY CAN EVEN TAKE U MORE DOWN. We have to forget the 5 senses to open intuition & see God. Course there r times wen we have to touch body or tense. But it is better to just walk naturally or move naturally which does not take one down usually. Stretching takes one down.

If we usually concentrate at the Spir Eye & r not aware of lower magnets, we may b 6th Up. If we want to achieve the 7th we raise the ener by concentration so that we can stabalize in the 7th. If our concentration is on vice, we can b sure that we have magnets in the lowers.

w lower magnets, we must keep hands away from lower body to not enhance the down. Never point palm or the 3 biggest fings toward Spine(they coorespond to the 3 lower chakras). The neg ener in the lower 3 centers will radiate out the 3 big fings & also turn the palm ener neg. That neg ener can take one further down. These r immutable laws; how God works.

Down people have no sensitivity to their state. But Up people can tell. It is like testing & getting wrong results cause u r down.

Sometimes wen I cant test, I test maybe 50-90 sec. Then I close my eyes a few sec & then open them to retest. Many times it will test bad very quickly. Am then in a naturally relaxed state & it flows. Must b Up to have accurate results.

I need some food, cant find none for me.

>   But its poi, u see?

Cant just strain water. Where 's the nutrition? oh me!

>   But the store is m-t no food to b had.

>   No milk & no juice. All is bad.

>   Sow new seeds now. Sow, sow, sow.

The ground is fertile, u tested the whole store 3 days in a row

Even more s poi will b gone.

Just more sugar, fat & salt & poi cardboard that's s.

I dont eat that. Would make a mess.

B ye perfect is not just an imaginary edict.

Might as well filter water & fast w me.

Drink water for u see can strain & get Purity.

Im in the House just Thee I see.

The music is Heavenly & Im content.

Just a nagging thot that is hell bent.

Got plenty yolks for my Heart & Thee.

U could win a major battle, take ground tonight.

Just would take another pull up. Again fight, just fight.

This is wat the Saints do to build Their might.

Strong is desired, weak thots will flee. B w Me.

I could live ur words but how do I nix the might of the hungry memory?

At least hunger ketosis made flee.

The hunger is gone, is just the memory.

Why bring it back like yesterday? Rather offer it to Me

for I can eat poi, no mess for Our Crew.

We can take 10 or even 70 or 100%

More than 1 of Us to help u get thru.

Turn the dial. Miss d fray from yesterday!

Headache & stiff? Why get sick? The indigestion s will stick.

For I have much work I want done today.

WALT MES

Im breaking out. I just want to shout Im m-t, m-t of want, m-t. Im free!

I want to b tall & go to High School, u see?

No more dragging the bottom but thru the Heart,

The door to Thee ever & ever in the Living Room.

> U have a start.
>
> Come join Me; get ur College degree.
>
> Receive ur healings at the top of ur Spine.
>
> Ill make u tall, an Immortal Saint too.
>
> Then U can help others. Help people like u.